Polish Saber

The use of the Polish Saber on foot in the 17th century

by

Richard Marsden

Polish Saber:

The use of the Polish Saber on foot in the 17th century

by

Richard Marsden

Copyright 2013-2015, All Rights Reserved

ISBN 13 978-1-950626-07-6

Edited by - Keith Farrell
Formatted by - Henry Snider
Cover Art by - Henry Snider
Cover Saber by - Andrzej Mikiciak

Preface

HEMA stands for "Historical European Martial Arts." This is a strange hobby and passion that blends martial skills with academic ability. The treatises, manuals and traditions of European combat throughout the ages are being re-discovered and revived constantly by a vibrant, active and international community. In the world of HEMA, knowing how to perform a technique is no more important than managing to find mention of it in a source in the first place. However, some of these lost arts have been more difficult to revive than others.

The saber techniques of the 17th century exemplify arts that are difficult to recreate. Polish saber techniques of the same century are even more obscure, with no concrete manual from which to work, but rather a series of clues with which to piece together a system. In short, it is a challenge for anyone involved in this particular branch of HEMA.

A film caught my eye before I accepted the challenge. In the film *Potop* (*The Deluge*, based on the novel by Sienkiewicz), a duel takes place in the rain between the tall, impetuous and spoiled Andrzej Kmicic and the short, seasoned and noble Michał Wołodyjowski. In the mud and grime of a dreary village, the two characters clash sabers in a scene that is exciting and vivid. While cinematic, there was a level of authenticity to the duel that made it almost unique in the annals of film-history. As Kmicic fell to the ground, wounded but alive in the pouring rain, I wondered what a real, historical Polish saber duel would have looked like.

From movie, to research, to a quest to find talent all over the world, I threw myself into the task of understanding not only the Polish saber, but also Poland itself during the 17th century. There is no place quite like it. Poland stands as a great meeting place between the cultures of the East and West – yet always it is Poland. Few societies can adopt radically foreign ideas, costumes and notions, yet preserve their core identity like the Poles. The 17th century stands as a high-watermark for Poland, where it stood as one of Europe's largest and most prosperous nations, with a level of religious and ethnic tolerance and political freedom that outshone its more despotic rivals. It also was a period of endless, ruinous war that would set the country on the path toward failure, dissolution and ultimately partition between its neighbors.

Dueling on foot is where I decided to focus my research, and duels on foot were common enough during the time period in question. Alas, the details of such duels are limited, and information about techniques and style is sadly lacking. To divine what the Polish saber duel on foot was like, I had to reach out to other sources, to other writers and researchers, and to form a truly international team with the shared vision of bringing the art to life and presenting it to an English-speaking audience.

The task was intensive, and even now remains incomplete. There are more sources out there, but as is so often the case in HEMA, each re-creation is but the starting point for another, and not the absolute end. It is my supreme wish that this work will be the same, and that it should stand not as the final word on the subject, but rather as the impetus for further study and research on the Polish saber duel of the 17th century.

Richard Marsden

Phoenix Society of Historical Swordsmanship

HEMA Alliance

Contents

For

AJ Marsden

Pam Marsden

Phillip Marsden

Tyler Brandon

Michael Chidester

Myles Cupp

Keith Farrell

Dr. Jeffery Forgeng

Olek Frydrych

Jonathan Hill

Christopher A. Holzman

Daria Izdebska

Ksenia Kozhevnikova

Mariana López-Rodríguez

Jeffery Lord

Jessica Marcarelli

Kevin Maurer

RJ McKeehan

Jerzy Miklaszewski

Reinier van Noort

Jacob Norwood

Carlo Parisi

Cara Patterson

John Patterson

Joshua Pendragon

Lee Smith

Henry Snider

Przemysław Stolorz

Piermarco Terminiello

Miandra T. Thomas

Phoenix Society of Historical Swordsmanship
HEMA Alliance
Arizona Renaissance Festival

Without these translators, researchers and fencers, without Keith Farrell as editor and Daria Izdebska as our Polish expert, there would have been no project. My thanks for your hard work, input and dedication.

Ҕistory and Background

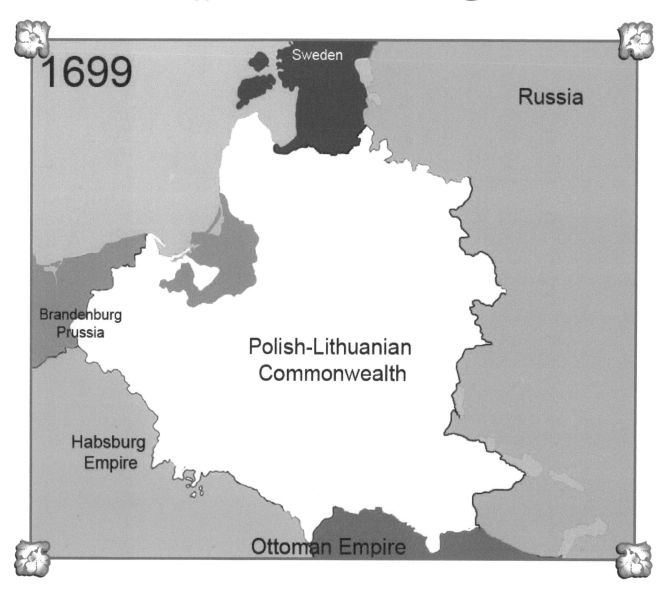

Poland on the eve of the 18th century: *despite a period of nearly fifty years of constant warfare, the Polish-Lithuanian Commonwealth remained largely intact at the century's close. The 18th century was far less kind and the Commonwealth would not survive it.[1]*

---

1   Esemono, *Poland 1699*, 2009, courtesy Wikipedia - public domain.

Europe in the 17th Century

The 17th century of Europe brought together the ideas and innovations of the Renaissance and saw them codified, perfected and expanded upon. Artists such as the Italian Caravaggio mastered the use of *chiaroscuro*: the extreme use of light and dark. Architects such as the Englishman Christopher Wren (in the wake of London's Great Fire) brushed aside medieval designs for new, classically inspired, baroque structures. The members of the German Bach family were already well known for their music, and their most famous son, Johann Sebastian, was learning the busy and complex sounds that defined the era. The French Sun King, Louis the XIV, embodied absolutism and would be admired and reviled by Europeans for almost half the century and part of the next. War was ever present.

The military revolution of the era, brought on by gunpowder, was nearly over according to Michael Roberts; it was ongoing, according to Geoffrey Parker; and it never happened at all, as theorized by John Childs.[2] Revolution or not, gunpowder dramatically changed how war was fought in Western and parts of Central Europe, and with keen, mathematical interest, these Europeans explored its use in the 17th century. Pitched battle was rare, and instead sieges and destructive forays were the norm. The new weapons of the prior century, namely the harquebus and cannon, were pitted against the complex fortresses designed by the likes of Vauban. Wars were fought not only for territorial gain, but also over religion, with the Thirty Years War in particular bringing ruin to the Holy Roman Empire and catapulting Sweden into the status of a major international power.

Warfare in the West was analyzed and manuals were written on how best to conduct it. Drill-books were created to detail the behavior of soldiery in the most simplistic way, such as the *Manuale Militare, Oder Kriegss Manual* (1616) by Johann Jacobi von Wallhausen.[3] The medieval method of individual nobles raising and training troops gave way to the state uniformly creating professional armies with their drill-books.

Example of baroque 17th century cannons. These heavy, bronze weapons were designed for siege warfare and were symbols of art, wealth, and raw power.[4]

2   John Childs, *Warfare in the Seventeenth Century*, (London: Cassell, 2001), 23.
3   Ibid, 139.
4   Adrian Velde, Design of two extraordinary 48-pounders cast at Lübeck by: Albert Benningck for Dutch States General in 1669, 1671, courtesy Wikipedia - public domain.

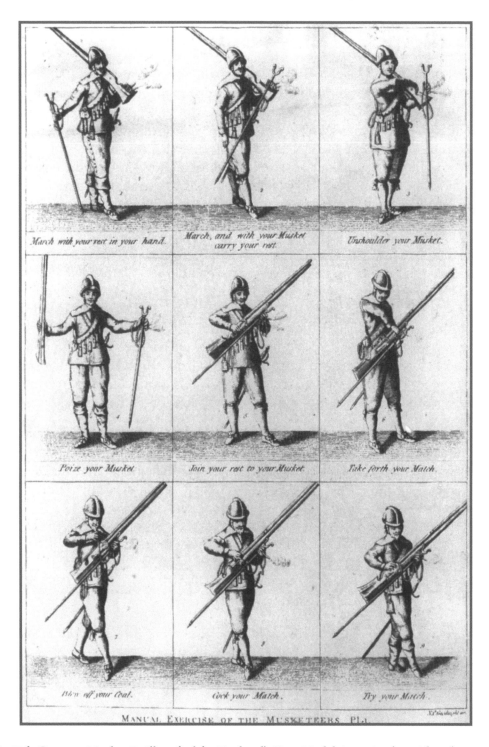

A 17th Century Musket Drill crafted for England's New Model Army in the mid 17th century. Such manuals were common in Western Europe and detailed the use of cavalry, gunpowder and pikes. They also detailed not just the design of fortresses, but also the best way to place such fortresses under siege.[5]

---

5   Mansell Collection, scanned from *A History of Warfare* by John Keegan. Original source unknown, courtesy Wikipedia – public domain.

Wars between states ran alongside warfare of a more personal nature. The nobility, eager to set themselves apart from common society, engaged in continual and violent struggle with one another. From the medieval trials by combat arose a formal (though often illegal) means of settling differences between gentlemen: the duel.

Politically, Western Europe was wracked by wars of religion and wars of absolutism. The ideas and notion of government and man's role in it were still forming. Clearly, by the 17th century, medieval feudalism had gone by the wayside – but what stood in its place?

In France, the absolutist Sun King held power. In England, the ambitions of Charles I led to his execution, and eventually to a rocky road toward Parliamentary democracy. The Age of Enlightenment was spawned by the excesses of the 17th century and would form the background of Hobbes, Locke, Rousseau, and Montesquieu.

Italy, for all its wealth, even with the Church in Rome and its profound cultural influence over Europe, was in a precarious position. Petty Italian kingdoms sat alongside equally petty and corrupt Italian republics. Italy's larger neighbors, such as France and the Holy Roman Empire, and with them Spain, were ever encroaching; no city-state in the peninsula could unite the other city-states, let alone oppose the larger powers.

The situation in Poland during the 17th century was very much different.

A panoramic view of Gdańsk (Danzig), Poland. The center of the city is medieval, but the walls are modern (by 17th century standards) and meant to withstand the cannons of the era.[6]

---

6   Pierre Aa, a copy of a 17th century sketch, 1729, Edmund Cieślak [ed:] Historia Gdańska 1655-1793, vol. 3, Gdańsk, 1993, courtesy Wikipedia - public domain.

Poland's Politics in the 17th Century

In the 1600's, the Thirty Years War rocked Western Europe, but not Poland. Western European monarchs emulated the absolutist Louis XIV, but Poland did not. Western Europe created drill-manuals for modern, state-run armies; Poland did not.[7] Western Europe favored infantry, and again, Poland did not.[8] Poland was profoundly different and unique compared to its Western neighbors.

During the 17th century, Poland was one of the largest and most populous nations.[9] It had relative religious and ethnic tolerance, unrivaled anywhere in Europe, and the most liberal of governments where the nobility (the *szlachta*) elected the king through a parliament known as the *sejm*.[10]

The Polish state in the 17th century consisted of several territories fused into one body known as the Commonwealth. Poland and Lithuania had been allied since the marriage of the Lithuanian King Jagiełło and the Polish Queen Jadwiga. Their marriage, and the Union of Krewo, culminated with the defeat of the Teutonic Order in 1410 and the establishment of a strong, Catholic state. Parts of Prussia and the Ukraine were added to the joint kingdoms, leading to contention with neighbors such as Muscovy. The last king of the Jagiellonian dynasty, Sigismund II, fused Poland and Lithuania into one entity, but at a great cost. Many concessions were made to the *szlachta* for their support, and the dual-kingdom of Poland and Lithuania became a single republic in 1569 with the Union of Lublin.[11] The term for Poland was *Rzeczpospolita Polska*, which roughly translated into the "Polish Commonwealth". Poles, Lithuanians, Tartars, Jews, Cossacks, Ruthenians, Prussians, and visitors from as far away as England and France all called the *Rzeczpospolita* their home.

The diverse ethnic and religious nature of Poland set it apart from its more homogenous neighbors. Tensions within the Commonwealth were surprisingly low during the early part of the 17th century. During the Thirty Years War, while Western Europe (and most notably the Holy Roman Empire) was shaken to the core, Poland was relatively untouched by the conflict and remained both Catholic and yet mostly tolerant toward its populace.

One of the curious features of the *Rzeczpospolita* was its elective monarchy. The *szlachta* had the right to assemble at the *sejm* and pick their monarch. The results of the election could be (and in the 17th century often were) contested. Tremendous power was left in the hands of the plentiful nobility, ensuring what they called their "Golden Freedoms."[12] Furthermore, the nobles could routinely

---

7   Books about military theory, rather than drill, did exist in Poland. Jan Tarnowski published *Consilium Rationis Bellicae* as advice on how to fight the Turks. Norman Davies, *God's Playground*, (New York: Columbia University Press, 1982), 122.

8   By the end of the 17th century, Poland's army had four horsemen per foot-soldier. John Childs, *Warfare in the Seventeenth Century*, (London: Cassell, 2001), 96.

9   The Walters Art Gallery, *Land of the Winged Horsemen*, VHS, prod The Walters Art Gallery, (Baltimore, Video, 1999).

10   Lonnie R. Johnson, *Central Europe*, (New York: Oxford University Press, 1996), 108-109.

11   The term republic should not be equated with how it is used in the United States today. The republic of 17th century Poland was applicable only to the nobility. That said, nowhere else in Europe did as many people have as much say in their government.

12   The Polish nobility in the 17th century made up 9 percent of the population, while in Spain and Hungary it was 5 percent, and in France only 1 percent. Norman Davies, *God's Playground*, (New York: Columbia University Press, 1982), 215.

stifle the power of the king through the *sejm*. The policy of the *sejm* was that of *Nihil Novi*, meaning "Nothing New," and this was used to keep the monarch weak. In particular, the king's army was prevented from becoming too large, and the most powerful nobles were given the right to raise their own troops. Nowhere else in Europe did such a large percentage of the population have such power over its ruler. A single voice of dissent could halt a *sejm* and was known as *Liberum Veto*.[13] When votes were taken, it was unanimous approval or nothing. The nobles were not required to perform military duty for the king, and it was up to each individual to determine when and how they became involved in politics and national defense.[14] The most powerful magnates ruled their estates freely, while the less prosperous *szlachta* were indebted to such individuals rather than to the king.[15]

In 1572, the last male king of the Jagiellonian dynasty died, leaving only female heirs. The youngest of these heirs, Catherine, was married into the Vasa family that united Finland and Sweden. The eldest heir, Anna, was married to Henry of Valois of France. The *sejm* approved Henry to be the new king, only for him to flee his throne and instead claim the crown of France upon his brother's death.

Chaos ensued as the *sejm* met again in 1575 to elect another king. The Holy Roman Emperor Maximilian II Habsburg was chosen, but the Polish *szlachta* threatened civil war and did not want to see the Commonwealth consumed by an authoritarian Imperial line, or involved in Imperial wars with Turkey. A new *sejm* was convened and it was decided that Stephen Báthory would marry Anna of the Jagiellonian dynasty and rule as king. In 1576, Báthory sat over an unruly Poland. The *sejm* that had elected him had been called in haste, and the Lithuanians preferred the prior candidate, Emperor Maximilian II.

While the rights of the *szlachta* were enshrined, there was no strong rule of law in the Commonwealth, and Stephen Báthory was faced with extreme difficulties in keeping his throne.[16] Anna had no children with him, Maximilian was loath to give up his claims to the throne, and foreign powers threatened Poland during her time of instability. Masterfully, Báthory led Poland's riotous and strong-willed people to new heights. The Polish populace was pacified with a reorganization of the laws and tax-structure.[17] Upon Maximilian's death, Báthory made peace with his heir, Rudolf II. The long-time enemies to the south, the Ottomans, were dealt with by a truce, and the Commonwealth's forces were marshaled to oppose the invasions of Ivan the Terrible from Muscovy.

Báthory's death in 1586 was sudden and it plunged Poland into another period of *sejms* and debate among the *szlachta*. There were more invalidations and internal conflict. The Habsburgs revived their claim, only to be thwarted by Sigismund III, King of Sweden and heir to the Jagiellonian dynasty through his mother Catherine. He was the first of the Vasa kings of Poland.

---

13   Ibid, pg 345.
14   Ibid, pg 215.
15   The Radziwiłł family grew so powerful that during the Deluge, Bogusław Radziwiłł betrayed the Commonwealth in the hopes of increasing his family's position with a Swedish alliance.
16   While the Commonwealth had the concept of legal precedence and liberties for its nobles, the king often had to fight his own people to bring rival factions into line. For example, rebellious nobles routinely challenged the *sejm*'s decisions. Lonnie R. Johnson, *Central Europe*, (New York: Oxford University Press, 1996) 10.
17   Báthory granted the power of the *sejm* to approve knighthoods, thus preventing the king from "packing" any election. Gdańsk (Danzig) was granted near autonomy. The right to elect the king was acknowledged in perpetuity. Declaration of war and the ability to use a military draft was left up to the *sejm*. Ibid, 237, 272, 334.

A.*Sacra Regiæ Maiestas* . B.*Archiepis: Gnesnen Primas Regni* . C.*Archiepis:LeopolienD.Episcopi Senatores* E.*Palatini, Castellani Senatores* . F.*Magistratus et Officiales Regni et Magni Ducatus Lithuaniæ : Senatores* G.*Officiales Curiæ Aulici et Secretarij R:S:M: H:Nobiles Regni et Mag.Duc.Lith.*

Iacobus Laurus f. 1622. Roma cu Priuilegio Summi Pontificis

The sejm meeting under the reign of Sigismund III. The massive body of nobles continually thwarted the dreams of Polish monarchs about strengthening their rule.[18]

Sigismund's rule was unsteady. He had claimed the Commonwealth as his own in 1587, but in 1599 he lost the Swedish throne to his uncle, Charles. Charles had raised Swedish fears that the Commonwealth's staunch Catholicism would threaten Protestant Sweden. Remaining in Poland, Sigismund attempted to reclaim his Swedish throne and also increase his royal authority over the Commonwealth. The King quickly found himself at war, not only with his uncle, but also with his own *szlachta*, who violently opposed any attempts at an increase in the power of the crown. Victory over his enemies in battle was accomplished, but with no lasting gains. Sigismund never regained the Swedish throne and he never pacified the Polish nobility.

Władysław IV was elected as the Polish king by the *sejm* in 1633 after the death of his father Sigismund III. Like his father, Władysław was also unable to achieve his goals. The Swedish throne remained unattainable, and while rebellious Russian Boyars had elected him as the Tsar of Muscovy, Władysław was unable to make good on the claim. Meanwhile, the *szlachta* continued to be as independently minded as ever and were suspicious of any attempts at an increase in royal authority. During their reigns, both Sigismund III and Władysław IV were patrons of the arts and sciences and they brought Western influences to the Commonwealth, including Western fashion and military changes.[19]

Without any legitimate heirs, the death of Władysław IV left the throne in the hands of his half-brother, John Casimir II. Despite spending years abroad, he was elected king by the fickle *sejm* in 1648. From his election as king until his abdication in 1668, John Casimir presided over a tumultuous Commonwealth. Poland faced numerous wars, including a massive invasion by Sweden (known as the Deluge) and a war with Muscovy, as well as an ultimately successful rebellion in 1648 by Zaporizhian Cossacks led by Bohdan Chmielnicki.

The Deluge in particular caused tremendous damage to the Commonwealth, including a loss of

---

18   Giacomo Lauro, *Polish Sejm under the Reign of Sigismund III*, 1622, courtesy Wikipedia - public domain.
19   The adoption of Western technology in the Royal Army, including muskets and cannons, took place under all of the Vasa kings. Still, the vast majority of Poland's army was mounted and relied on the lance. John Childs, *Warfare in the Seventeenth Century*, (London: Cassell, 2001) 117.

cultural works that were transported to Sweden as war-booty, as well as a drop in population from the continual and destructive conflict.[20] John Casimir abdicated his throne, but even in the act of leaving he wounded Poland. Casimir took with him valuable art to France where he lived out his days as a Jesuit in exile, adding to Poland's cultural loss during his reign.

A 19th century depiction of John Casimir taking an oath before God at Lwów Cathedral to drive the Swedes from the Commonwealth.[21]

Bohdan Chmielnicki with Tugay Bey.[22]

A Polish noble claimed Bohdan's family estate. Bohdan appealed directly to King Władysław IV and was given a royal charter securing the land. The Polish noble took away Bohdan's estate anyway, and the King was powerless to prevent it.

Exiled from his ancestral estates, Bohdan rallied the oppressed Cossacks of the Ukraine into open rebellion in 1648. When he died of natural causes in 1657, the Ukraine had broken away from Poland and found itself under Russian influence instead.

---

20   The Deluge and subsequent wars ruined Poland. Nearly every city was sacked, sometimes more than once! Norman Davies, *God's Playground*, (New York: Columbia University Press, 1982), 315.
21   Jan Matejko, *Oath of King Casimir*, courtesy Wikipedia - public domain.
22   Jan Matejko, *Bodhan Khmelnytsky with Tugay Bey*, courtesy Wikipedia - public domain.

Michał Wiśniowiecki was the next to be elected by the *sejm* in 1669 and bore no link to the old Jagellionian line. His claim to fame was mostly the result of his father, a feared commander who earned his reputation trying to put down the Zaporizhian Cossacks. After a generation of near-continual warfare, the Commonwealth was in a sad state, and under Michał's reign found no fortune.

Jan Sobieski, known as John III, was elected by the *sejm* in 1676 and did much to repair and rebuild an ailing Commonwealth. Popular and adventurous, he rallied the divided population in a war with the Ottomans. When Vienna was besieged in 1683, it was the Polish hosts of Sobieski that descended into the Turkish camp and drove them from the city's walls. It would be the last time the Ottomans put Vienna under siege and, ironically, it marked the decline of both the Polish Commonwealth and the Ottoman Empire.

Although he was able to save Vienna, Sobieski was unable to press far into Ottoman territory, and upon his death in 1696 many of the problems of the past monarchs still remained.

Jan Sobieski blessing his troops before riding to the relief of Vienna in 1683.[23]

23   Juliusz Kossak, *King John III Sobieski*, 1871, courtesy Wikipedia - public domain.

The final monarch to claim the Polish throne during the 17th century was an outsider. Augustus II, a Saxon elector, was made king by the *sejm* in 1697. Like many kings before him, he sought to rein in the *szlachta* and had dreams of turning the Commonwealth into an absolutist monarchy. Augustus the Strong (named so for his physical prowess) proved no more successful than the previous kings in his attempts.

The 18th century saw the gradual weakening and finally the violent dissolution of Poland. It was partitioned, against its will, among its more organized and absolutist neighbors: Prussia, Russia and Austria.

The Szlachta and Sarmatism

It was not unusual for the nobility in any society to mark themselves as different from the commoners. This could be through style of dress, laws, marriage restrictions, as well as legal rights and privileges. The idea that the nobility was somehow a breed apart from the rest of society lent credibility to their favored status. In Poland, the noble class was numerous, and its members were by no means all wealthy,[24] but they were all powerful. As a whole they decided, through the *sejm*, who would be king of the Commonwealth, and they kept the king's power in constant check. During the 17th century they formed a society of equals, bound by customs, a culture of horsemanship, legal privileges and a belief in a separate ethnic identity, different from that of the commoners.[25] Jealously, they guarded their "Golden Freedoms."

The *szlachta* believed themselves to be descended not from a Slavic origin, but from Eastern horsemen called Sarmatians, whose origins were in the lands around the Black Sea. It was this mythical Eastern lineage that brought not only the Eastern style of dress into fashion, but also a separate cultural identity that was enforced by various Polish historians.[26] It was Sarmatism that made the unique Polish clothing popular among the nobility. They wore a long tunic called a *żupan*, a loose-sleeved coat called a *delia*, a baggy robe called a *kontusz*, and wore long sashes around the waist – all of which were elements of Sarmatism. Compared to most Europeans, the *szlachta* had an exotic and Eastern appearance.

Key among their fanciful dress was also the saber, or *szabla*. Just as Western knights valued their swords, wearing them long after their military value diminished, so too did the Polish *szlachta* prize their curved blades.

Additionally, Polish hairstyles were often Eastern in style. Shaved heads and long moustaches ran counter to the long hair and trimmed beards of the West.[27]

The fashions of the *szlachta* were not set in stone. As in Western Europe, fashion changed constant-

---

24   Polish nobles could be as poor as peasants or wealthier than the king. The Lithuanian Radziwiłł family was noted for living in better conditions and possessing more land and palaces than the king. The Walters Art Gallery, *Land of the Winged Horsemen*, VHS, prod The Walters Art Gallery, (Baltimore, Video, 1999).
25   Simon Schama, *Landscape and Memory Vintage*, (New York: New York, 1995), 38.
26   Sulimirski Tadeusz, *The Sarmatians* (New York: Praeger Publishers 1970), 167.
27   Richard Brzezinski, *Polish Armies 1569-1696* (1), (London: Osprey Publishing, 1987), 7.

ly, often from year to year.[28] When Sobieski's army drove the Turks from Vienna, they entered the enemy camp clad in Hungarian attire, complete with eagles and leopard skins. When they exited the camp, they had a distinctly Ottoman appearance, and merrily adopted their enemy's dress as their own.[29]

Jan Pasek, a Polish noble of the 17th century, complained bitterly about the ever-changing styles and the sheer cost of remaining fashionable. In good humor, Pasek noted that it would take 10 ox hides to write down all the adopted fashions of Poland. He claimed that clothing meant to last a lifetime would be discarded within the year in the name of remaining fashionable.[30]

Frivolity with money, not unknown among European nobility, was lauded among the culture of Sarmatism. While on parade, Polish nobles affixed golden horseshoes to their steeds in a loose manner. As the horses trotted, the golden shoes fell off, letting the spectators see not only the dazzling wealth of the *szlachta*, but also their flippant disregard for it.[31] The use of gold and silver and fanciful dress, even on military campaign, was a source of frustration for the Polish monarchs. King Stephen Báthory passed laws and regulations in an attempt to limit the display of wealth within a military camp, but the rule of law was not strong in Poland and the king's decrees were ignored.[32] Fashion trumped the will of the king![33]

Patron polski.

AVOCAT POLONAIS.

The *szlachta* were numerous in the Commonwealth, and a majority were not landowners. By law, if not in practice, the poorest noble was equal to the wealthiest magnate. Custom dictated that nobles referred to one another as "brother", and the *sejm* was curtailed from using any titles that might place one noble's status above another.

Rich or poor, the *szlachta* of the 17th century were noted for their education. The fluent use of Polish and Latin, often together, impressed foreigners.[34]

Their power was perhaps too supreme, and the 17th century revealed a weakness: the *szlachta* had power, and sometimes wealth, but no civic duty. When the Commonwealth was threatened, the decadent *szlachta* were not always there to answer.

Polish attire depicted in a 19th century work. The Polish Patron wears a red żupan, and over it a blue delia. A golden sash is wrapped around his waist while a saber hangs faithfully at his side.[35]

28   A Polish chronicler noted that within a span of 10 years, fashion had been influenced by Russia, Sweden and Turkey – coinciding with conflict with these countries. Ibid, 8.

29   Ibid, 44.

30   Jan Chryzostom Pasek, *Memoirs of the Polish Baroque,* translated by Catherine S. Leach (Los Angeles: University of California Press, 1976) 52.

31   Richard Brzezinski, *Polish Armies 1569-1696* (1), (London: Osprey Publishing, 1987), 8.

32   Ibid, 7.

33   Stephen Báthory once said sarcastically that those from Gdańsk/Danzig shot golden musketballs! Norman Davies, *God's Playground*, (New York: Columbia University Press, 1982), 286.

34   Ibid, 237.

35   Jean Pierre Norbin, *Polish Patron*, 1817, Bibliothèque nationale de France, courtesy Wikipedia - public

The Winged Hussar

Most of Poland's military was mounted, and the heavy cavalry were known as the Winged Hussars.[36] The Winged Hussars in the 17th century wore metal armor of an Eastern and Western design and sported large wings on their backs. The origins of the wings are unknown, but may have come from Serbia or Hungary.[37] Armed with long, hollow lances, as well as sabers and a variety of other weapons, the Winged Hussars were a terror on the field. They were a unique military unit whose behavior and imagery impressed Poles and foreigners equally.[38]

Winged Hussar armor of the mid-period. In the background lies the Constantia, which depicts an early-period Winged Hussar on parade in 1605.[39]

"So mightily he smote then that I felt my own sword shudder in my hand; I withstood the first encounter."
- Jan Chryzostom Pasek

domain.

36   Richard Brzezinski, *Polish Armies 1569-1696* (1), (London: Osprey Publishing, 1987), 10.

37   Ibid, 14.

38   Ibid, 10 (French and Polish commentators referred to the Hussars as beautiful and impressive).

39   Bazylek100, *Polish Hussar's Half-Armor*, 2011, courtesy Wikipedia - Creative Commons Attribution 2.0 Generic.

Religion

Poland had a level of religious tolerance matched by few other places at the time. Poland did not partake or suffer in the Thirty Years War, and just under 50% of the populace was Catholic in 1660.[40] Catholics, Jews, Orthodox Christians and Protestants and even Muslims lived together within the vast borders of the Commonwealth. This was achieved by enshrining Catholicism as the main religion, but safeguarding, and in some cases enriching, minority religions. There were no forced conversions, no massacres, and no civil war as had occurred in Western Europe. Yet, religious differences seeped into the Commonwealth's patchwork of ethnicities and political interests.

Jews, for example, held a particular place in the Commonwealth by serving as managers for the nobility. Jews had their own assembly in the government and a level of autonomy unheard of elsewhere.[41] This earned them the ire of the rest of the population who saw them as privileged tax-collectors.

When Chmielnicki led his successful rebellion of the Ukraine, the Orthodox faith, as well as the Ukraine's Cossack heritage, were factors beside his personal grudges.

The city of Danzig, like the Ukraine, had ethnic and religious differences with the majority of the Commonwealth. Their Protestantism as well as their German roots eventually brought the city under the sway of Prussia.

King Sigismund III temporarily ruled both Sweden and the Commonwealth, only to find that Poland's religious tolerance was not shared by his homeland. Swedish fears of Poland's Catholicism prevented any long-term unity between the two.

Still, for most of Europe, the 17th century was one wracked with religious war. Not so in Poland.

---

40   Norman Davies, *God's Playground*, (New York: Columbia University Press, 1982), 162.

41   Ibid, 440.

Eastern Influences

Poland in many ways was a "Middle East" of the Baltic. Just as the Middle East found itself wedged between Western Crusaders and Mongol incursions, so too did Poland face similar threats and cultural influences.

In 1453, Constantinople fell to the Ottomans, marking an end not only to Byzantium, but also to any credible Crusade from the West. In 1410, Poland-Lithuania defeated the Teutonic Knights, and in their own way retired the notion of the Western Crusade.

In 1258, Mongols from the East put Baghdad to the torch. Seventeen years before, they had done the same to Kraków. Both the Ottomans and the Poles suffered under the Mongol threat; both eventually survived, and incorporated elements of their mutual invaders.[42]

Perhaps fittingly, the Ottomans and the Commonwealth bordered one another in the 17th century. After the fall of Hungary to the Ottomans, the Commonwealth took on the title of "the Bulwark of Christianity," while the Ottomans saw themselves as the successors of Islamic expansion. While there was much saber rattling between the two, and some war, trade was also common.

Poland likely adopted the curved saber from the East in the 16th century. They also took to Eastern clothing, such as the wearing of broad, colorful sashes. After Sobieski's rescue of Vienna, the booty from the Turkish camp changed Polish fashion overnight!

Sarmatism looked to Polish origins in the East, and interaction with Russia was continual. Perhaps the East influenced Poland more in the 17th century than at any other time in history.

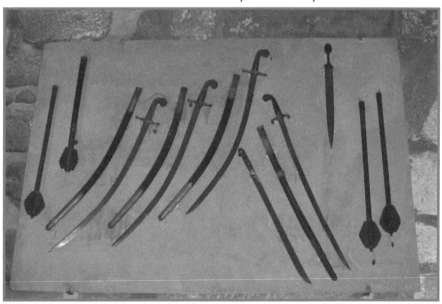

A variety of Turkish weaponry. Poland during the 17th century used similar weapons, ranging from the saber to the mace.[43]

---

42   A catch-all phrase for the numerous Mongol groups was Tartars.

43   Georges Jansoon, *Turkish Swords*, 2007, courtesy Wikipedia - Creative Commons Attribution Share-Alike.

Western Influences

Well before the creation of the Commonwealth, Poland had Western influences, in a large part from Germany. The port-city of Danzig was known in Poland as Gdańsk. In the 15th century, Gdańsk had joined with Poland as an autonomous zone after warring with Poland's old rival, the Teutonic Knights. Despite being more German than Polish, Danzig and 20 or so other Prussian communities remained part of the Polish Commonwealth, quite voluntarily, until the partitions in the 18th century.[44]

The rise of the Vasa kings in the 17th century brought to Poland a great influx of Western ideas, in terms of both military and fashion. Traders and craftsmen from the West traveled to Poland. Italian notions, including those of the duel and the use of the rapier, were adopted. Strong ties were made with England in the wheat trade, while French fashions were imported alongside Turkish and German.[45]

Poland's military also adopted certain Western customs. The Polish army incorporated pike and shot tactics to augment their numerous cavalry. The Vasa kings in particular encouraged a level of Westernization in Poland, leading to a foreign contingent within the Commonwealth's royal army,

44   Jeanry Chandler. Interview with Richard Marsden. Facebook Interview. Phoenix, July 3, 2013.

45   Sobieski's Wilanów palace had Polish, French and Italian features. The Walters Art Gallery, *Land of the Winged Horsemen*, VHS, prod The Walters Art Gallery, (Baltimore, Video, 1999).

known collectively as "German."[46]

The crossroads of East and West can often be found in Poland, and this explains the eclectic nature of the region. Only in Poland would one find a palace with Italian gardens, a French interior, being visited by noblemen wearing Turkish sashes, sporting Eastern mustaches, while wearing Western boots.

The Duel in Europe

Private warfare among the nobility had long plagued Europe. While officially frowned upon by the Church and only haphazardly approved by the State, the duel existed in some fashion or another for quite some time. Among the Vikings, the duel took place between men with sword and shield, in what was known as *holmganga*. Medieval Danish custom allowed affairs to be settled on roads outside of town. Trial by combat in Western Europe was given some checks and balances in the Lombard Laws from 713-735, but persisted until the 16th century.[47] However, the State (French, English, Polish or otherwise) gradually withdrew its support of legalized combat between men. In 1547 in France, the death of the court favorite, François deVivonne, sieur de La Châtaigneraie, at the hands of Guy Chabot Baron de Jarnac, turned the king Henry II's stomach enough to outlaw trial by combat.[48] In 1559, the very same king was killed in a friendly joust, causing that particular sportive form of "duel" to fall out of fashion as well. The Council of Trent (1545-1563) specifically demanded that all Catholic countries renounce judicial combat in the hope of curtailing the duel.[49]

Despite these regulations, men of note continued to fight one another over their notions of honor in a more private and often illegal setting. The use of armor ceased, as did the lengthy formal requests

---

46   Richard Brzezinski, *Polish Armies 1569-1696* (2), (London: Osprey Publishing, 1987), 6.

47   V.G. Kiernan, *The Duel in European History*, (Oxford: Oxford University Press, 1989), 33.

48   Ibid, 37.

49   Ibid, 47.

to the State to sanction combat. Men of equal station and high birth could, with the aid of seconds, challenge one another to combat. The duel would be arranged, usually outside the view of the public, and could consist of a fight to the first touch – or could extend to a duel to the death.[50] As trial by combat and jousting faded away in the mid to late 15th century, the personal duel replaced it.

The rise of the personal duel coincided with the production of treatises about dueling, and also detailed descriptions of how weapons should be used in a duel. The Italian city-states propagated both the *Code Duello* and manuals of arms. Antonio Manciolino's *Opera Nova* of 1531 detailed the use of several weapons, including sword and buckler, which could be used by a gentleman in war, for self-defense, and in an affair of honor.[51]

Later Italian manuscripts, such as Nicoletto Giganti's 1606 treatise, depicted the use of the rapier: a long and slender weapon, better suited for civilian defense and dueling than for warfare. These rapier manuals, and with them a fascination with dueling, spread well beyond Italy's borders.

In England, the Italian master Giacomo Di Grassi taught the use of the rapier in the late 16th century. This was much to the annoyance of more traditional gentlemen such as George Silver, who saw the weapon, and the practice of dueling with it, as murderous.[52] The Italian fencer Salvator Fabris had his works printed in Denmark, and he was spoken of highly throughout Europe.[53]

Sebastian Heussler, a German, produced his own book on the use of the rapier, and was influenced both by Salvator Fabris and by another Italian, Ridolfo Capo Ferro.[54]

In Poland, the notions of the duel found a welcome (though not entirely studious) audience.

---

50   Ibid, 47.

51   Antonio Manciolino, *Opera Nova*, translated by Tom Leoni, (Wheaton: Freelance Academy Press, 2010), 1.

52   George Silver, *Master of Defence: The Works of George Silver,* translated by Paul Wagner, (Boulder: Paladin Press, 2003).

53   Fabris traveled throughout Europe as a fencing instructor and was employed at one time by the King of Denmark. Tom Leoni's translation of Fabris' works remains as a stellar example of Italian rapier-theory.

54   Wiktenauer, http://wiktenauer.com/wiki/Sebastian_Heu%C3%9Fler accessed 6-17-2013.

The Duel in Poland During the 17th Century

The duel was immensely popular in Western Europe, to the point where France occasionally lost more men to dueling than it did to wars.[55] However, the duel in Poland was forbidden by the Church and regulated by the State. If the power of God and monarch were not enough, the lawsuits resulting from duels curbed their practice.

During the Middle Ages, the *szlachta* had a legal means to announce their displeasure toward a fellow nobleman. A challenge was written and it was known as the *odpowiedź*. It was not a challenge to a duel in the Italian sense, but rather a declaration of war. The *odpowiedź* would be delivered to the district court, and the aggrieved noble and his men would seek out battle. This was not a one-on-one duel with matched weapons, but rather a brutal battle, in which it was acceptable to burn a rival's crops, kill his peasants, and attack his friends and family. In the 17th century, few nobles announced their private wars so openly and the *odpowiedź* was rarely used. Ambushes and nighttime raids were the preferred methods.[56]

Single combats with sabers on foot did take place, but were informal by Western standards. Additionally, it was rarely fatal, with a single wounding cut usually ending the affair and bypassing the legal matters that a death was sure to bring.

Customs and rules were often set in place, such as restrictions on dueling while on campaign, and were duly ignored by the willful *szlachta*.

---

55   V.G. Kiernan, *The Duel in European History,* (Oxford: Oxford University Press, 1989), 74.
56   Norman Davies, *God's Playground*, (New York: Columbia University Press, 1982), 352-353.

For example, a nobleman called Pasek fought two guests at a party in a military camp, and then fought the host. Dueling was not allowed within the military camp, but that did not stop Pasek, nor was he punished for it. All involved were well into their cups and no one died as a result. The host of the party was fined, and Pasek, being a sporting sort of person, paid for the surgeon who was needed for the wounded guests.[57]

Another time, Pasek struck a man in the presence of King John Casimir. This was a grave offense, punishable by death. However, Casimir cheerfully pardoned Pasek for his transgression.[58]

When Pasek was formally challenged to a duel, in the Italian fashion or with an *odpowiedź*, he decided not to wait for a time and place to be agreed upon, but rather rode out to his rival's home and demanded they fight then and there. Pasek didn't mention if he rode out alone, or with a host of friends at his back. His foe declined to fight and peace was made between the pair.[59] Pasek's haphazard attitude towards dueling was not unique to him, and was even shared by royalty.

Foreigners were often baffled by the Polish lackadaisical attitude toward the rules of dueling. An Italian traveler visiting the Commonwealth found himself at odds with Prince Zboruski. The Polish prince idled away his days by tormenting the Italian visitor. The Prince coated the traveler in honey and had bears lick him clean. He took the wheels off the Italian's wagon so that his victim could not leave, and he devised various means of embarrassment for his trapped guest. Frustrated, the Italian challenged Zboruski to a duel.

The Prince, familiar with the Italian etiquette of dueling, noted that only men of equal station could challenge one another. He declined the duel. Furiously, the Italian researched his genealogy, and had papers shipped to him to prove that he had a noble lineage. He presented the documentation to the Prince, with all the glee of a lawyer, and once more demanded a duel.

Zboruski acknowledged the paperwork and the hard work of the Italian, and still refused a duel, choosing instead to harass the man some more! The rules were only guidelines that Polish nobles followed capriciously.[60]

The causes for a duel remained fairly universal in Poland and throughout Europe. Any perceived insult was grounds for a fight. Pasek, for example, fought over ill words, a shove, and preferential lodging. More often than not, alcohol was involved beforehand.

While laws and customs were routinely ignored, if a duel went too far, a man would find himself in serious trouble. Wounding an opponent in a duel, at the worst, could result in a fine. Killing a man, depending on his family's wealth and influence, could result in lengthy and expensive lawsuits that could go on for years, and could lead to long-lasting vendettas.[61]

---

57   Jan Chryzostom Pasek, *Memoirs of the Polish Baroque,* translated by Catherine S. Leach (Los Angeles: University of California Press, 1976), 60.
58   Ibid, 153.
59   Ibid, 78.
60   John Gideon Milligen, *The History of Dueling,* (London: Samuel Bently, 1841), 358.
61   In 1588 the murder of a nobleman (by another) resulted in a fine of 240 groats and 54 weeks in a dungeon. Enforcement was usually up to the aggrieved, not the Crown. Norman Davies, *God's Playground,* (New York: Columbia University Press, 1982), 235.

In a fight over lodging, Pasek wounded a man gravely. Pasek was deeply concerned, not over the man's ultimate well-being, but about the lawsuits his death might bring, going so far as to note that it was easier to slip out of town than a dungeon.[62] So costly and pervasive could a lawsuit be that battle cries during personal scuffles included, "To sword!," "Slay them!" and "Take him to Court!"[63]

Despite only a nominal adherence to the rules of dueling and the fear of lawsuits, duels did occur in Poland during the 17th century. Duels were generally fought on foot with sabers, but could be conducted on horseback as well. As in the Italian tradition, perhaps mimicking it, witnesses stood by while the participants fought. Fatalities were not common, but grievous injuries were. Zabłocki, after researching a variety of 17th century diarists, five out of nineteen duels were ended due to a strike to the head, while fourteen ended with a strike to the hand, resulting in such colorful phrases as "loose fingers".[64]

Strikes to the hand could be terribly damaging but were survivable. During the reign of Sigismund III, Tomasz Saphiea lost his hand in a duel to Jerzy Zenonowicz. Minus a hand, but unperturbed, he went on to have a successful military career.

Kitowicz noted that at the raucous *sejm*, dueling with sabers resulted in hands removed, cheeks wounded and heads dented, but that once blood was drawn the duel ended.

The weapon of choice was generally the saber, but in sudden and impromptu duels, whatever was on hand would suffice.[65] Kitowicz, in his observations, stated that the duel with the saber was much preferred, because with the war-hammer death was almost certain.

While Italians wrote down the rules for dueling, and wrote detailed manuscripts about how to fight with the rapier in duels, Poland had nothing similar. There was no recognized dueling code in Poland until 1919, though most likely the Italian *Code Duello* was nominally accepted during the 17th century when single combat was sought.[66]

There are no known detailed Polish texts on the use of the saber until well after the 17th century. However, there are hints at a Polish "style" of combat that, like Polish culture, was probably influenced by outside forces.

> "It was said that even at home, being in his cups, he has music played, and he performs various fencing maneuvers, now thrusting, now parrying, on and on, till he drops from weariness. An expert fencer was he, so they say."
> - Jan Chryzostom Pasek discussing Chledowie

62   Jan Chryzostom Pasek, *Memoirs of the Polish Baroque,* translated by Catherine S. Leach (Los Angeles: University of California Press, 1976), 161.

63   Ibid, 164.

64   Wojciech Zabłocki, *Ciecia Prawdziwa Szabla*, (Warsaw: Wydawnictwo sport i Turystyka, 1989), 18.

65   One of Pasek's opponents in a sudden duel was armed with a rapier rather than a saber.

66   http://literat.ug.edu.pl/honor/ accessed 7-23-2014. The "Polish Code of Dueling" was written by Władysław Boziewicz.

FACING PAGE - Piotr Skarga gives a sermon to King Sigismund III (seated) and powerful magnates (standing center). The man whom Skarga may have decried the most was Stanisław Stadnicki (the man to the left of the person wearing gold). Stadnicki was known as the "Devil of Łańcut" and after serving with valor in the Commonwealth's wars, decided to retire to a life of legalized banditry. He claimed an estate as his own, and used torture, murder, raids and extortion to enrich himself at the expense of travelers and nearby communities. Attempts to sue him resulted in an odpowiedź and punitive raids. A favorite tactic of his was to print and distribute insulting documents about fellow szlachta, who in turn would declare an odpowiedź or simply seek him out. When they tried to attack Stadnicki, he would defeat them and take their riches. In 1608, Stadnicki insulted the wrong man and his castle was stormed by Łukasz Opaliński. Stadnicki fled, but two years later was killed in an ambush while attempting to reclaim his lost lands.[67]

Training

Poland did not have fencing schools in the same way as in Italy. There are, for example, no period-texts from Polish saber-masters instructing students or illustrating their techniques. Instead, the use of the saber was most likely taught through the use of the single-stick, known as a *palcat*, by Jesuit priests and other educators.[68] The game of *palcaty* was played not only by children but by adults as well.[69]

---

67   Jan Matejko, *Skarga's Sermon*, 1864, courtesy Wikipedia - public domain.

68   The Commonwealth was just under 50% Catholic during the 17th century, and the Jesuit schools were well known, but few in number. *Palcaty* was most likely taught by whatever schooling a nobleman received. Norman Davies, *God's Playground*, (New York: Columbia University Press, 1982), 162.

69   The word *palcaty* is both the plural for *palcat* and the name of the single-stick game.

The Saber

The Polish saber was primarily a sword meant for mounted combat, though it could be used to settle issues of honor, love, country, politics, or be drawn during drunken festivities. The famous Polish noble Pasek found his saber in hand for numerous duels, or near-duels. The most spectacular such event was at a party, where he dueled with three people.[70] The shapes of 17th century Polish sabers differ, but they share certain characteristics that affect their use.

CURVED

Polish sabers have varying degrees of curve in the blade. The curve maximizes cutting potential, and so on horseback, sabers were excellent weapons. On foot, the saber is no less deadly, and although designed for the cut, it can still perform a thrust. The curved nature also allows for the ability to stab around parries, thus requiring parries to be more exaggerated to guard against this kind of action.

LIMITED HAND PROTECTION

A defining aspect of Polish sabers is that they offer very little by way of hand protection. Simple cruciform shapes were common, sometimes with a chain stretching from the quillon to the pommel. Other variations offered more protection, with a floating knuckle-bow and/or thumb-ring being popular. The thumb-ring offered limited protection for the thumb against vertical strikes but provided additional control of the sword, while the floating knuckle-bow protected the front of the hand. Shells and full knuckle-bows replaced these in later periods.

---

70   Jan Chryzostom Pasek, *Memoirs of the Polish Baroque,* translated by Catherine S. Leach (Los Angeles: University of California Press, 1976), 60-62.

Parts

The saber can be broken down into simple parts.

Hilt = The hilt of the saber can be shaped like an eagle's head or can be straight.

Guard = The guard includes the quillons and any other additional pieces such as a knuckle-bow, thumb-ring or chain.

Blade = The blade of the saber is curved and may flare out into what is called a *yelmen*. The portion of the blade closer to the guard is called the strong, because it parries well. The portion of the blade closer to the tip is called the weak, because it does not parry well. Ideally, parries are performed with the strong, and attacks are made with the weak. The edge facing the opponent is called the true edge, and the "back" of the sword is known as the false edge or spine.

Types

Wojciech Zabłocki in 1989 classified Polish sabers in his book, *Cięcia Prawdziwą Szablą*. He placed sabers into lettered and numbered categories.

Saber type I is known as the Hussar Saber. These sabers have closed hilts, in the form of a kunckle-bow, and thumb-rings.

Saber type II is known as the *Karabela*. They have an eagle-pommel, and are without thumb-rings or knuckle-bow.

Saber type III is known as the Hungarian Saber. They are noted for their *yelmens* (flared blades), thumb-rings and an open hilt, but sometimes had a chain strung from the quillon to the pommel to act as a knuckle-bow.

Saber type IV is known as the Polish Battle Saber or sometimes as the Armenian Saber,[71] although Zabłocki described it previously as the Tartar Saber.[72] They have open hilts and pistol-shaped grips making them similar to the Cossack *szaszka*.

The numbers were assigned a letter, which further classified the shape of the weapon in question. A type IIIA saber, for example, has an open hilt, while a type IIIB has a chain acting as the knuckle-bow.

---

71   It was probably of Tartar origin and was used by Tartar units in the Polish army. Wojciech Zabłocki, *Szable świata*, (Warsaw: Wydawnictwo, 2011), 79.

72   Wojciech Zabłocki, *Ciecia Prawdziwa Szabla*, (Warsaw: Wydawnictwo sport i Turystyka, 1989), 89.

WEIGHTS

Zabłocki detailed the weights of several 17th century Polish sabers:[73]

IA *Batorowka* saber in the Warsaw Polish Military Museum	= 2.1 lbs / 0.95 kg
IA saber in a private Krakow collection	= 1.9 lbs / 0.86 kg
IA saber in the Warsaw Polish Military Museum	= 1.4 lbs / 0.64 kg
IA + ID saber in the Warsaw Polish Military Museum	= 1.96 lbs / 0.89 kg
IIA saber in a private Krakow collection	= 1.7 lbs / 0.77 kg

BLADE LENGTHS

Zabłocki also measured the lengths of blades:[74]

IA *Batorowka* saber in the Warsaw Polish Military Museum	= 34.5 ” / 87.63 cm
IB saber in the Krakow National Museum	= 36 ” / 91.44 cm
IA + IC saber in the Warsaw Polish Military Museum	= 32.3 ” / 82.04 cm
IIC saber in the Dresden Armory	= 28.9 ” / 73.41 cm
IIIB saber in the Warsaw Polish Military Museum	= 33.5 ” / 85.09 cm

Similar to the Polish saber was the British 1796 Light Cavalry saber, a sword that had limited hand protection and a steep curve. Clearly, the weight and length for this style of weapon had changed very little from the 17th century to the Napoleonic Wars, as different models of saber from different countries across the centuries exhibit the same sort of characteristics.

1796 British Light Cavalry Saber   Blade Length = 33” / 83.82 cm   Weight = 1.7 lbs / 0.77 kg[75]

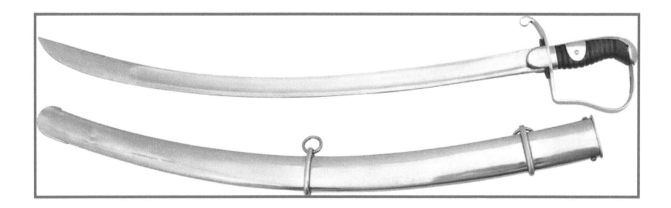

---

73   Ibid, 116-342.
74   Ibid, 116-342.
75   Replica by Cold Steel.

Types of Swords used in Poland 15th - 18th Century[76]

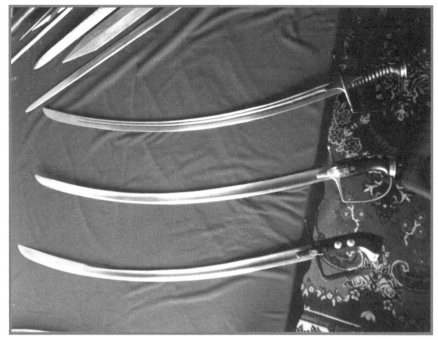

Top = Hussar Saber ID Early 18th century
Middle = Hussar Saber IA Late 17th century
Bottom = Hussar Saber IB Middle-Late 17th century

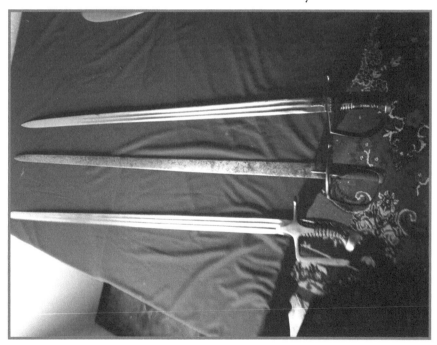

Top = Pałasz Early 18th century
Middle = Pałasz Late 17th century
Bottom = Pałasz Middle-Late 17th century

76   Replicas by CCS Silesia.

26

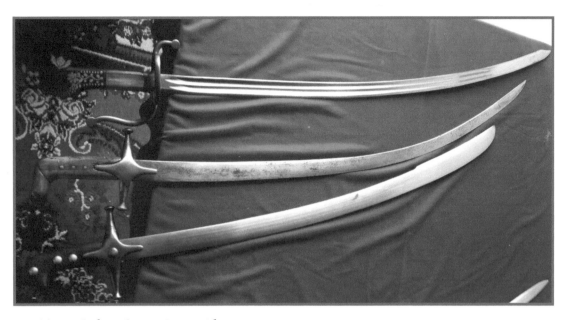

Top = Italian Storta Late 16th century
Middle = Shamshir Late 17th century
Bottom = Turkish Karabela IIB Middle-Late 17th century

Top = Hungarian IIIB Late 16th century
Middle = Jan Henryk Dąbrowski's Pałasz 18th century (Replica of original)
Bottom = Pałasz Middle 17th century

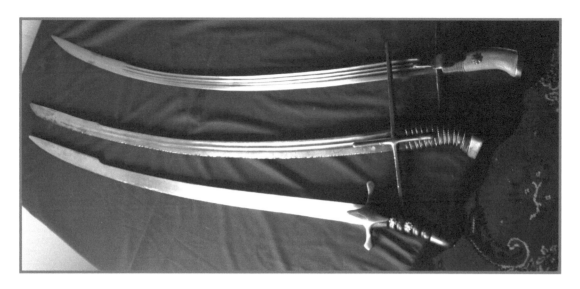

Top = Hussar IA Early 17th century
Middle = Hungarian IIIB Late 16th century
Bottom = Hungarian saber Early 16th century

Left = Hussar saber Type ID
Middle = Hungarian saber Type IIIB
Right = Karabela Type IIB

Text Sources

There are few concrete sources on the use of the Polish saber. However, by piecing together the various clues available, an idea can be formed as to what the system may have looked like in the 17th century. There are some Polish texts, some 17th century Italian texts, some 16th century German works, and some later period connections as well.

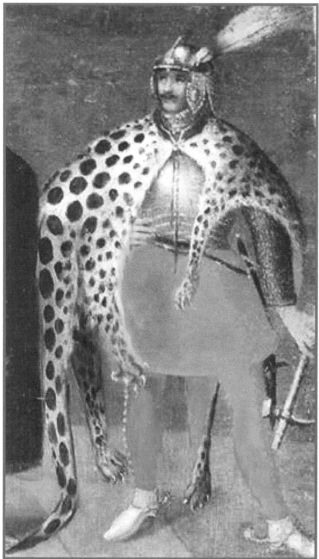 

Left: Polish attire in 1620. The hussar wears Western spurs, sports a leopard-skin coat, and beneath it wears a župan. In his hand he holds a war-hammer called a nadziak.[77]

Right: Polish attire in 1630. Though only ten years separate the pictures, the fashion had significantly changed.[78]

---

77   Anonymous, *Fellow Hussar*, circa 1620, courtesy Wikipedia - public domain.

78   Dollabella Tomasso, *Portrait of Stanisław Tęczyński*, circa 1630, courtesy Wikipedia - public domain.

Polish

POLISH TEXT BY JAN PASEK

Jan Pasek (1636-1701) wrote down his memoirs in which he colorfully depicted the times, troubles and culture of Poland during the 17th century. Pasek was a *szlachcic*[79] of the Commonwealth and earned for himself fame and infamy in equal parts. His memoirs were not printed until the 19th century and they describe many violent confrontations as well as Polish attitudes toward dueling and fencing.

Catherine Leach, translator of Pasek's memoirs, noted that Pasek's view of history has to be looked at with a level of skepticism. His sense of humor is supreme, but his accuracy is not. Pasek saw himself as a heroic figure, and is depicted as such throughout his memoirs.

When it comes to fencing, specificity is lacking. Given that Pasek wrote his memoirs at the end of his life, it is understandable that he did not recall with perfect clarity the nature of his fights and duels from thirty years ago. Still, there are clues to be found.

Pasek used words like "clash," indicating that swords did meet and touch when fencing. He also makes references to withstanding assaults and having his saber shiver in his hands. In duels, he targeted fingers and hands, and in war would thrust when having to kill a man quickly. Pasek never mentioned training, or even practicing with the saber, except in the case of a curious host at a party.

The following are paraphrases and small quotations from Catherine Leach's excellent translation, *Memoirs of the Polish Baroque*.

---

79   Nobleman.

"MEMOIRS OF THE POLISH BAROQUE"

[excerpts]

by

Jan Chryzostom Pasek (1636 – 1701)

English Translation: Catherine S. Leach

"THREE DUELS IN A DAY"

Pasek was with the army and drunk at a party. He was provoked by two other equally drunk men, the Nuczynski brothers. They desired to fight, but Pasek didn't have his sword and he noted that dueling while in the camp was forbidden. His fellow *szlachcic* could not be dissuaded and so Pasek retrieved his saber and obliged them, one after the other.

> *"He (Nuczynski) takes a swipe at me and saying: "You'll die." While I'm saying: "God decides that." On the second or third thrust, I struck his fingers and I say: "So you see, you've gotten what you asked for." I thought he would content himself with that. He, being drunk, either did not feel it, or perhaps wanting vengeance, attacks me again, brandishes his sword once, twice, blood now splattering upon his face. When I slice across his pulse,[80] he collapsed."*

> *"The younger brother flies over, starts slicing thick and fast. God looked down on my innocence. We clash: both his hands and sword dropped."*[81]

After Pasek defeated the pair, the host of the party, Jasinski Marcyjan, demanded a duel as well. He guided Pasek toward a narrow river with planks across it so that they could fight outside the camp.

> *"He (Marcyjan) shoves me ahead on those planks: "Go in front, you! No sooner do I step upon the plank, but he slices from behind at my head, but the Venetian velvet was excellent and the Lord preserved me, it didn't cut through, save in one place the velvet gave way a little, and beneath only a red welt as from a whip lash..."*

> *"So mightily he smote then that I felt my own sword shudder in my hand; I withstood the first encounter. We clash a dozen times; neither side gaining the upper hand. I say: "Enough of this Pan[82] Marcyjan." He says: "You son-of-a-so-and-so, you've not done a thing to me and you've had enough." No sooner did he speak his reproach, but the Lord so designed, that I cut him across his cheek with the very tip of my sword, and leapt away from him. Now does he strike out at me even more; when I wound him in the head, he loses his footing. Then, taking my sword in both hands, I began striking him with the flat side, forcing him to the ground."*[83]

---

80   Fingers, wrist, or hand.

81   Jan Chryzostom Pasek, *Memoirs of the Polish Baroque,* translated by Catherine S. Leach (Los Angeles: University of California Press, 1976), 61.

82   The word *"pan"* means "Sir."

83   Jan Chryzostom Pasek, *Memoirs of the Polish Baroque,* translated by Catherine S. Leach (Los Angeles:

Fifteen duels were fought that day. Pasek said he won his three because of the Lord and admonished his readers about dueling. In duels that he provoked, Pasek said he was always defeated. In duels where he was the one provoked, he claimed he was always victorious. Pasek paid for the surgeons for the Nuczynski brothers, while Marcyjan was fined for letting the party get out of hand.[84]

"Lodging Dispute"

Pasek and several of his men entered the town of Wilno, which was crowded with *szlachta* and their men for a meeting. Lodging was scarce, and so Pasek and his men claimed a half-built house as their own. Political meetings were dangerous affairs.

> *"No assembly took place without a tumult, uproar, and drawing of swords."*[85]

> *"There being robbings and assaults night and day, I had my men stand guard..."*[86]

While in the half-built house, Pasek encountered seven drunken townsmen who were upset with him staying there. The house had a frame and little else, and within were Pasek, his men, his horses as well as the seven belligerents! Within these crowded confines, a fight ensued when one of the townsmen tried to untie Pasek's horses and drive them from the house. In the following fight, Pasek referred to clubs, rapiers and seemed to be using a saber. There is some indication that some of his assailants had no weapons at all!

> *"The townsman dashes to untie the horses, but my man clubs him in the chest, he fell. To sword!"*

> *"When that uproar started, one Lithuanian, having become embroiled, leapt out of that sword-play among the horses; I had a chestnut horse, shamefully swift- now does my chestnut strike out with hooves. And that one fell. Two down."*

> *"We're outside- now at each other! My boy watching my rear, two men hard by me. Somehow they beat the boy away from me: one ripped at me from behind, but not very much, and he jumped aside at once. At the same time, the townsman fell down in the nettles; he not having been hurt, in an instant my men jumped in front of him with rapiers, and he got up. He rushes straight at me slashing with all his might; I withstood it, then having deferred, I slashed him across the pulses; nothing; onward to cut and thrust."*[87]

> *"There's my boy smiting his attendant on the noggin; down he went. His lordship attacks me once more; I slice across his fingers again: the rapier drops, he takes to his heels."*[88]

University of California Press, 1976), 61-62.
84   Ibid, 60-62.
85   Ibid, 159.
86   Ibid, 159.
87   "Pulses" is described as the underside of the wrist, where the pulse is taken, in Giganti's contemporary work. Aaron Taylor Miedema, *Nicoletto Giganti's The School of the Sword,* (Kingston: Legacy Books Press, 2014), xxv.
88   Jan Chryzostom Pasek, *Memoirs of the Polish Baroque,* translated by Catherine S. Leach (Los Angeles: University of California Press, 1976), 160.

The rest fled and later in the night, Pasek was confronted by other townsfolk asking to know who he was. Fearing that one or more of the attackers might have died, Pasek did not reveal his true name. While stating boldly that he would give satisfaction to anyone who chose to fight him, secretly he worried.

> *"God forbid that one of them should die! Although they would release me, yet the procedure itself of a lawsuit, the court investigations, the cost, etc. I think how to slip away from that place, for previous court verdicts had already taught me it's easier to make your way out of a forest than to get out of prison."*[89]

"Ignored Protocol"

Pasek was challenged in the Italian fashion to a duel, and as was so often the case in Poland, rewrote the rules.

> *"A certain grand gentleman challenged me to a duel, indicating through responsible persons*[90] *that he was determined to kill me. So I, without waiting for that uncertain hour, preferred to choose it myself, the speedier to be rid of the thought rather than fear longer. I rode into his courtyard and dispatched a boy to announce that "my master, whom your Lordship has declared he will kill, not wishing your Lordship any ado in seeking him all over the face of the earth, and before he grows any thinner, has come and herby gives notice of his presence." That gentleman did not kill me; he restrained himself and apologized."*[91]

"The Somber Swordsman"

While traveling, Pasek and his companions came upon the estates of Tomasz Chledowie. Due to bouts of madness, Chledowie did not live with his wife, who had agreed to play hostess for Pasek and those with him. Pasek described Chledowie with a mix of awe and pity, and it is the only time Pasek mentioned training. Of the many people Pasek met, the Castellan of Zakroczym was given one of the more lengthy descriptions.

> *"...a decent person he (Chledowie) was, an old soldier, tested and true, save for being touched in the head, that's why they (he and his wife) lived apart from each other, having borne only one daughter. "*

> *"When sound, he was a man of such valor, that all feared him."*

> *"Once he trounced Karol Potocki's squadron in the first encounter, they at their full strength, himself riding out with ten cavaliers and explaining to them "not in my village, lest you'll be saying I'm confident in a crowd; but I'll wait for you in the open field." and so he did. When*

---

89   Ibid, 160-161.
90   This would indicate seconds.
91   Jan Chryzostom Pasek, *Memoirs of the Polish Baroque,* translated by Catherine S. Leach (Los Angeles: University of California Press, 1976), 78.

both sides had assembled, he challenged the lieutenant who rode out of the squadron."

"To sword!" The Castellan charged, smote him hard twice, and the man fell from his horse. Whereupon the entire squadron attacked him; he stood his ground then, and with his own suite set about subduing them: he sliced them to bits, slaughtered them, took their standard and drum, and sent it to the hetman."[92]

Pasek noted that Chledowie's madness made him pious and quiet. He sewed a crucifix to his cap. At times, he'd remove his cap and stare at the crucifix intently, and his servants said the man had never laughed. A page followed him around carrying his sword.

Pasek and his men dined with Chledowie's wife, and only once did Chledowie arrive. He was friendly, but humble, choosing to take a seat that was lower than that of his wife and guests.

"At times his (Chledowie) discourse was to the point, at times point-less, and the sword right beside him with the boy, whereon I kept a sharp eye, a madman after all, being a touchy matter."[93]

Drink was had, and musicians arrived. Soon there was dancing and good cheer, but Chledowie would have none of it. He drank, and said nothing, eventually choosing to leave. One of Pasek's companions tried to stop him.

"Why does Your Lordship not partake of our good cheer in your own home?"

He, striking his sword with two fingers, replies: "I've grown used to dancing with this maiden alone; were I to dance with her in battle array, it might make things unpleasant for someone."[94]

Having suitably squashed any argument, Chledowie rode off. Pasek revealed a final anecdote about the somber swordsman.

"It was said that even at home, being in his cups, he has music played, and he performs various fencing maneuvers, now thrusting, now parrying, on and on, till he drops from weariness. An expert fencer was he, so they say."[95]

> "Thus, at the crack of dawn the Marshall, right in front of the earth-walls surrounding the stronghold of either the Castellan or the Voivode, would let the young boys fight each other with sabers, or with lances, if they had their mail on."
> - Michał Starzewski discussing training

---

92   Ibid, 57.
93   Ibid, 58.
94   Ibid, 58.
95   Ibid, 55-58.

Polish Text: Father Franciszek Salezy Jezierski

Born to a noble family, before becoming a priest, Jezierski was a soldier in the Commonwealth. He served as deputy commander in the Golden Lance, a unit of hussars, and fought against Ukrainian bandits called Haidamaks, who plagued the Commonwealth. After the Partition, he fought against the Russians up until the 19th century.

After soldiering, he became a preacher and prolific writer, decrying the outrages of his own noble class and the plight of the peasants and burghers. In the 18th century, Father Jezierski provided a snippet of valuable information on the nature of saber fencing that perhaps he had picked up during his time as a hussar.

> *"It seems that, just as merriment has its own outward ways of expression, where the national character is exhibited in various dances, so the movements resulting from anger influence the ways one uses steel. The Hungarian cuts from the left, the Muscovite from above, the Turk towards himself, and the Pole uses cross cuts."*[96]

The quote provides clues to general saber fencing techniques as well as national preferences.

The Hungarian and Russian cuts are easy enough to interpret.

Bartosz and Janusz Sieniawski (researchers and theatrical performers as well as historical fencers) believe that the Turkish cut was fully incorporated in Poland and was the "Hellish Polish Fourth" described in Starzewski's 19th century diagram.[97]

Jezierski's commentary that Poles use cross cuts remains mysterious. The most straightforward interpretation would be two cuts, the first from one direction, and then the second from the opposite direction. However, there are no solid period Polish pieces of text dealing with the saber that define the cross cut any further, and numerous 19th century Polish descriptions are vague and well-removed from the 17th century. Still, these later-period pieces refer to the *Sztuka Krzyżowa*, the "cross cutting art," and that in and of itself is telling.[98] Variations of the cross cut can be found in dussack manuals of the 16th century and in Giganti's 17th century second book on the rapier as well as a reference to the Polish fight and cross cuts in Henning's brief instructions on cut-fencing. Together, they provide the most simple of interpretations: a cut from the right followed up by one from the left.

96   Translated by Daria Izdebska.
97   Bartosz Sieniawski and Janusz Sieniawski, translated by Daria Izdebska, HROARR: http://www.hroarr.com/the-sabers-many-travels-the-origins-of-the-cross-cutting-art/ accessed 4-3-2013.
98   One article noted that after the Napoleonic Wars Poles still knew the cross cutting art, but by the 1860's it had been lost. Ibid.

Polish Text by Jędrzej Kitowicz

Jędrzej Kitowicz detailed the martial customs of Poland during the reign of Augustus the Strong, who ruled from the final years of the 17th century well into the 18th century. While very late-period for the purposes of this book, Kitowicz wrote about what were clearly long-standing traditions that were in place throughout the 17th century and perhaps even before that.

The game of *palcaty* was used at an early age to teach children the value of swordsmanship. The game consisted of fencing with a stick and was taught at Jesuit schools, with even the teachers taking part according to Kitowicz. For adults, the game could involve others as well, including those just passing by. Sparring with single-sticks that bore no basket, while the players were entirely unarmored, would surely teach some key fundamentals that could be applied to the Polish saber. Two fundamentals can be drawn from Kitowicz's account.

First - The hand had to be kept safe. Polish sabers had only limited hand-protection, while the *palcaty* had none at all! A few rounds during a game of *palcaty* would teach the value of keeping the hand safe, as well as limberness and dexterity.

Second - Physical size and power did not give any intrinsic advantages. Kitowicz described how the tall and strong Saxon guards of the king were no match for the smaller Poles who engaged them in a more dangerous version of *palcaty*.

Another aspect about the saber, which can be gleaned from Kitowicz, is that the use of the saber in a duel was rarely fatal compared to the use of a Polish war-hammer called a *nadziak*. Duels with the saber were still dangerous, but tended to halt after the first blow was stuck; or as Kitowicz noted, "One would cut off the other's hand, or wound his cheek or dent his head, and so the blood thus drawn from the adversary would hold off further fierceness and violence."

Kitowicz's account provides insight into the use of the saber and also its cultural status within the Commonwealth. The following excerpts detail the most salient points.

> "So mightily he smote then that I felt my own sword shudder in my hand; I withstood the first encounter."
> - Jan Chryzostom Pasek

"On Customs and Traditions in the Reign of Augustus III"

[excerpts]

by

Jędrzej Kitowicz (1728 – 1804)

English Translation: Daria Izdebska

On Bringing Up the Children

On games played by students

Palcaty: The second game during break time [at school] was fighting with wooden sticks called *palcaty*[99] where two students would bout with each other. This practice was crucial, especially to the nobility, because it taught and prepared the youths for future use of the saber, a practice which helped our ancestors achieve great things during various wars. Those fights were truly a sight to behold. When two students started playing with sticks, they would be at it until they became exhausted. They handled their sticks so deftly and with such art, blocking and guarding from all sides, and responding with a blow at their opponent, that neither one nor the other could hit the face nor head nor the sides. And there were already such masters among them that they taught and coached all the others. Occasionally, even the younger professors, both Jesuits and Piarists, would fight splendidly with the sticks. Thus, *palcaty* were in common use by students not only during the time devoted to breaks in the school day, but even in the schools themselves, right before the lesson started. If a student was too frightened and did not have the courage to face another, he had to suffer much abuse and mocking from the entire school, and he would often get bumps on the head or belting over the back.

On the Customs of the Nobility

On attire, or garments

It was not proper for a burgher to go about with a saber, with the exception of the inhabitants of Kraków, Poznań and Vilnius –because of their age-old privileges.

A nobleman buckled on a saber whenever he would leave the house, and took a horseman's war-hammer in his hand (pol. *nadziak*, but also *obuch*[100] and *czekan*[101]). It was constructed like so: a shaft one inch thick in diameter, long enough to reach a man's waist from the ground. At the end that would be held by the hand, it had a round silver or brass knob. At the other end there was a flat iron hammer, fixed firmly to the shaft. One of the ends of that hammer, the flat end, was similar to a shoemaker's hammer. The other end, if it was flat like a small axe, was called a *czekan*; if it was pointed and thick and slanting somewhat, then it would be a *nadziak*; and if it would be rounded like a bagel, it was called *obuch*.

---

99   A singular term would be *palcat*.
100   A war-hammer.
101   A war-hammer.

It was a terrible tool in the hand of a Pole, and even more so at the time when there was so much inclination and will for brawls and squabbles. When the nobles would use a saber, then the matter was different. One would cut off the other's hand, or wound his cheek or dent his head, and so the blood thus drawn from the adversary would hold off further fierceness and violence. But a wound dealt by a *nadziak* would often be deadly, yet without any sign of blood. Thus the one who dealt the blow would not cease in his attack, as he could not see blood, but would beat upon his adversary even more, breaking ribs and fracturing bones, without leaving a trace on the skin. The nobility who used the hammers would often deprive their victims of health and sometimes even life. This is why it was forbidden to appear with a hammer at all the political gatherings (i.e. *sejms*, *sejmiks*[102], tribunals), which was when the brawls and fighting would take place most often. Also, in the cathedral in Gniezno, there is a sign on the largest door that warns all those who would enter the House of God with such a villainous implement that the curse shall be upon them. It was truly a villainous implement, because if one hit the other with the sharp end of a *nadziak* right behind the ear, one would kill him instantly, driving the fatal iron right through the temples.

The saber, at the time of King Augustus III (1734-1763), was quite varied. The simple black saber (that is, in an iron sheath on leather straps) would be most common among the poor nobility. Instead of cap or *kursz* [two types of leather used for the sheaths – probably goatskin and calf-skin], sheathes would be bound with eel skin. It did not really matter with what it was bound, because it was the blade (the iron) that was worthy of respect. And not only among the poor nobility, but even among the most wealthy of nobles, the saber was passed down from father to son, from the father's son to the father's grandson, and further down the line, together with the most precious of stones and jewelry. The black saber was always carried by all manner of brawlers, night-prowlers and troublemakers, who found their fun in cutting people or leaving saber marks on the faces of some foppish youths, or even chasing a German in white stockings right through mud. Most often, however, the black saber was used in any and all circumstances in which there might be a chance for unrest and fighting. Those who were dressed in a German fashion would usually take a German *pałasz*[103] or a double-edged rapier. Additionally, the black saber was used for dueling – the most common weapon in these circumstances.

The old-fashioned black saber always had a curved blade. The best sabers were produced by the Wyszynski saber-makers. They were tested rigidly. A good saber should bend so that the tip of the blade can reach the very pommel and then spring back to its original shape. Later, straight sabers became fashionable, as did *staszówki* [sabers made in Staszów] and the straight and light Spanish blades, which did not hang as heavily around the waist but were good for protection and self-defense. The hilts on black sabers had an angular hilt-guard, also known as the cross, and a thumb-ring for the thumb. Later, when *sejms* and tribunals became more and more tempestuous, such hilt for the saber were developed that could protect the entire hand. Such a hilt was called a *furdyment*[104] or a basket and it consisted of several iron bars that covered the hand like a cage, and a large piece of iron plate.

To balance the proportions of such a large hilt the sheaths were as wide as a plank, even when

---

102   A smaller, localized *sejm*.

103   Generally a straight sword, but in Old Polish could refer to a saber or dussack.

104   A basket.

very thin sabers were put into them, from which the fashion spread to all sabers – even those that did not have baskets. This fashion, which did not last for very long, originated in Lithuania, and the Crowners [i.e. Poles] have adopted it from there. However, there must have been a similar fashion even in the Roman Republic, when the Latin poet – I don't know which one, Horatio or Martialis – wrote this verse: "*Grandi in vagina, Pontice, claudis acum*", which means: "In your large sheath, Pontic, a needle is contained."

Sabers with wide sheaths and large hilts were mostly used by courtly men, those without prudence or judgment, brawlers, and those who loved to slash at each other with swords in taverns and villages. Whosoever they would beat, they would also rob blind, or he had to pay a ransom to them if he did not have the strength or courage to fight. Soon, however, because such a weapon is heavy and destroys the clothes, the custom was set aside. Strangely enough, it was set aside when more peaceful times followed after the rough and violent times. Together with more elegant dress one would wear a Turkish *karabela*[105], a Tartar *czeczuga*[106] or a *pałasik*[107] decorated with silver or gold or oil-blackened. Such swords were most often brought from Lviv and accordingly they were called *lvovian*.

The saber and *karabela* were slung in two ways: the most ancient method favored broad leather straps with buckles and silver or gold terminals at the end. These straps held the saber at the waist so that the crossguard would be at waist-height. The straps would go around the waist only on the left side and would be tied in the middle of the small of the back at waist-height. *Rapcie*[108] would be tied in a similar fashion. They were similar to straps, yet not made of leather, but of a silk cord, often plaited with gold and silver, sometimes made entirely of gold and silver. Courtiers, fancy men and young nobles would color-match their *rapcie* for saber or *karabela* with their żupan (traditional dress of a Polish nobleman).

No one worried about the color of the straps, though. Later, the saber would be tied in a "longer" fashion, so that it hung under the knee and it was necessary either to hold it by the hilt whilst walking or to carry it under arm, so that it would not get between the legs and trip the wearer. The straps and *rapcie* went around the entire back like a harness on a horse. This fashion – silly and extremely uncomfortable – did not last for more than five or six years. It was abandoned and men returned to the short and narrow suspension that did not cover the back at all, but just the side. This was also not very comfortable, because the saber would smack the wearer on the side whilst walking.

On Soldiers

On the Crown Foot Guard

The Crown Foot Guard did not select the men according to their height. They recruited everyone who wanted to serve, even the shortest of people, as long as they were not blind, lame or hunch-

---

105   A type of saber, originally brought over from Turkey, it later became a typically Polish saber, often heavily ornamented and used as part of a nobleman's dress. It could be used as a weapon by removing the precious stones and the more flashy hilt.

106   A type of saber, Tartar or Kirgiz in origin, with a very slightly curved blade. Ornamental and worn with the Polish-style clothing just like a *karabela*.

107   A lighter version of the *pałasz*.

108   Elegant silken straps used to hold a saber at the waist.

backed. The Foot Guard was a haven for all thieves, cheats, wayward sons, wastrels and anyone who was forced to flee because of murder or another serious crime. They also took on various craftsmen from Warsaw, who were not allowed to practice their craft freely by the guild masters because they did not pay their guild fees. Whosoever of these took upon the raiment of the Guard was free from any prosecution or assault. There were good men in the Guard as well, whose parents or relatives recommended them for this novitiate in hope of a future promotion and general improvement. The last type of men were those who were abducted: handsome youths, butlers, ruddy peasants who had drunk a little bit too much in a wayside tavern and allowed a guardsman's hat to be placed upon their heads. After they had put it on, as if they had given the most solemn of oaths, without any other ceremony, they were taken away and brought to command as new recruits. The Crown Guard had the reputation of being the best soldiers, since the regiment was home to the most dangerous and shady of men, the outlaws and show-offs, who were ready for everything and who continually practiced hand-to-hand combat at various tribunals, meetings in Radom, and gatherings in Warsaw. No one was so skilled at putting down a fight, a battle, a bloody carnage, as those guardsmen. However, no other soldier was as quick and ready to look for a fight. The guardsmen would forever wander around all the drinking dens and bad company, looking for someone to taunt, so that they could later beat him up and strip him down – they were not deterred by the regimental fine or the possibility of a change of luck.

They found most leisure in teasing the royal drabant guard (a Saxon cavalry regiment that was made up the tallest and most handsome of men). The guards would tail the drabants like hunters following prey. Whenever the guardsmen would do battle with them, they would do bloody carnage upon the drabant. Most often, they would cut their faces, shamefully disfiguring the handsome men, their noses and cheeks cut through, the ears cut off. The only benefit of this was the doubtful glory for the guardsmen that they, as midgets, could defeat the giants. The king was sorely enraged with the officers of the guard and with their general that they could not keep their soldiers in check, so that his own drabants would not be so afflicted. He called upon the officers of staff and the general himself several times, complaining about the state of affairs and asking for a working solution. The general and the officers did whatever they could; they punished severely whomever they could catch. Finally, when nothing else was working, they decided that the guardsmen needed to be deprived of their *pałasz*, which all the soldiers on and off duty carried with them. At this time, however, the soldiers fixed their bayonets to their flintlocks only during drills and when they were part of a detachment. At all other times they carried the bayonets with them, next to their *pałasz*. So when the guardsmen were deprived of their *pałasz*, they started going against the drabant giants with sticks. They put their bayonets on the sticks and scarred the faces of the giants even more. The giants, who were very heavy men and not very good at saber, did not know a single fencing sequence, but always came at the guardsmen from above, as if using flails. In response the guardsmen came in underneath, quickly and smoothly, marked the giants on the face, then retreated.

King August seeing that at each drill there were more and more drabants with faces marked with signs [*paragrafy* – lit. articles of the law], sent them back to Saxony, and called on a regiment of *karwanierzy*, equally tall and massive as the drabants, but not as handsome. He did not care about them as much, and the guardsmen were not as eager to fight them as the previous ones.

On the Lawyers

On tribunals

To prove that you were of noble birth you did not need a genealogy. An old saber would do, often covered with eel skin instead of a sheath.[109]

[after some mocking and jokes] (…) sometimes the dispute would move outside the town, with sabers drawn to resolve it. But because it happened among friends and since those youths were not likely to hold grudges for very long, it was mostly hats and coats that suffered, not the bodies. And such duels often ended with glasses of wine, or jugs of mead, to toast the honor of knightly hearts.

On beating each other with sticks

Various lawyers and advocates would often meet outside the city hall after the tribunal was concluded. There they would fight each other with sticks, one-on-one, within a circle formed by the others. Those sticks were of various shapes and sizes, for young and for old, thinner and thicker, made of dogwood or oak – the thinnest (the thickness of a finger) were for young boys, and the thickest were for those who already had their moustache. These were thick as a staff or a peasant's cudgel. All of them were called *palcaty*. When everyone had their turn, the one who won against everyone else, or the one who was thought to be the best "player", became the Marshal of the circle; the second one in line, close in his art to the first one, became the Vice-Marshal; the third became the Instigator; the fourth became a Vice-Instigator [all those are names for the highest officials in the Commonwealth]. Thus, when they finally had their newly appointed officials, the entire noisy rabble went to the Jews (wherever those were). The Jews would then need to find special gifts for those newly-appointed officials and throw a feast for the entire band. The Jews did so instantly, not daring to disagree, and wishing to avoid the attack from those hotheads who, if not satisfied, would not let any Jew appear in the market without dragging him through the spokes in a wheel and lashing him on his cap and back. After the gifts and having feasted to the full (usually with mead, bagels and small breads), the band came back to the town hall. There the "stick jurisdiction" began, which lasted as long as the town's officials were debating and there was still daylight.

This jurisdiction spread over everyone who was equal in status to the members of the Circle, but sometimes even those who were above them in station, and who just happened to walk nearby the city hall when those of the Circle were showing off with vigor. Whenever a passer-by would thus imprudently pass next to them, he would be dragged into the circle and one of the members of this circle would come up against him. If the member of the circle managed to score a bump on his head or a welt on his face, then the passer-by was no longer forced to fight with anyone else. He would be congratulated that he became their brother, a guild-friend, and he lost simply by an unfortunate accident which happens even to the best of fighters. After that, he would no longer be dragged into the circle, but if he ever wanted to take part voluntarily, he had the right to do so at any time. If he managed to win against the first member of the circle, he was faced with

---

109   There is more to it than Kitowicz lets on. Nobles were a part of, or joined, a clan of nobles who bolstered one another's claim. Witnesses were required if a person's nobility was truly in doubt. Records were so few that the nobility referred to themselves as *szlachta oodwieczna* "the immemorial nobility." Norman Davies, *God's Playground*, (New York: Columbia University Press, 1982), 207.

a second, and then third, or fourth, always from the pool of the least skilled, until they got bored with him or he successfully implored to not fight again, or he gained the privilege of friendship and brotherhood. If the passerby would not wish to fight at all, he would be beaten with a stick on the head, lose his neckerchief or cap or a sum of money, with which he would buy himself out from this vexation. He would be free from the Circle's plays from then on, but he would not be granted the honor of camaraderie. Instead, he would gain an offensive title/name.

If the passer-by asked for the Marshal at the very start, the Vice Instigator stepped forward saying that he was not allowed access to the Marshal until he first fought his way up the ranks. If he was beaten by the first, second or third official, then he could no longer ask to fight the Marshal. If he did manage to defeat the first three, the Marshal would have to accept the challenge. If the current Marshal won, he would be applauded by the entire Circle and gain even more fame, but his opponent, after having defeated the lower ranked members, was not the lesser for it and could, if he so wished, take up the rank of the one he had defeated. If he actually managed to defeat the Marshal himself then he would be proclaimed the new Marshal by the entire Circle, and if he wanted to take up the office then they would all go to the next feast at the Jews (although it would be not as lavish). If he did not wish to take up the office, the previous Marshal would remain in his position, and the victor would leave, but graced with honor, fame and respect. He could also be invited to a customary drink by the defeated Marshal, after which they would sometimes play with sticks once again, and – as it often happens in these adventures when fortune turns around – the Marshal would regain his lost fame. Oftentimes, it would so happen that important courtiers, or great fencers of other sort would pretend to be cowardly or without skill, just for laughs. When they were dragged into the circle, they would beat the Instigators and the Marshal thoroughly and meticulously. The members of the Circle would quickly learn never to drag similar men into the fight again.

The Instigator and Vice-Instigator had several responsibilities. They would invite those youths and older men who passed by the city hall or looked upon the circle, dragging them into the circle, by force if necessary, with help from other members of the Circle. They would also act as seconds in the fights between the members of the circle, whether serious or in play, or with a new arrival. They also made sure that one would not cause too much harm to the other, nor use foul play or treachery. Additionally, they had to make sure that the fierceness born out of the stick fighting would not grow more serious and transfer to quarrels solved with more dangerous weapons outside the circle, but that the fierceness always ended within the circle by way of a mutual apology. The Marshal's duty was to arbitrate the more difficult feuds that were passed on to him by the Instigators. When the Marshal was not present, the Vice Marshall took his place. The custom of stick-fighting was not used solely at the tribunals, but also at regional and magistrates' courts.

Polish youths engage in a game of palcaty, while an elder with a nadziak on his shoulder watches.[110]

110   Martino Almonte, *Election Diet*, 1697, courtesy Wikipedia – public domain.

Polish Text: Michał Starzewski

The manual written by Starzewski is a source with strengths and weaknesses. It is in Polish, written by a Pole, and describes the use of the saber in the 17th century. However, the treatise was written in 1830, and is far-removed from the actual time-period the author purports to represent.

Starzewski's treatise was written after the Napoleonic Wars, when saber manuals were being gradually revised for sport, as modern weaponry made the sword less viable on the field of battle.[111] Looking at his treatise, there are indications that he was influenced by an overall trend toward faster but less-powerful cuts, a trend that was taking place during his lifetime. The techniques within Starzewski's work are fast, but lack power, and are closer aligned to modern fencing than martial applications. He was well-versed in the fencing of the day and had opened his own salle in Krakow, further supporting the idea that modern notions of fencing colored his view of fencing in the past.

Starzewski wrote not only about fencing techniques, but also about how a 17th century Pole shopped for a saber in the marketplace. There are no indications that this description is entirely accurate, nor his vision of 17th century Polish saber fencing. Further adding a shadow of doubt to his work is the use of fictitious words that were created to sound suitably ancient. The translator, Daria Izdebska, had to go to great lengths to divine Starzewski's intent.

Criticisms aside, Starzewski's treatise on fencing does give some good (and at times specific) rules for saber fencing, as well as the components and nature of the saber. Given that he wrote in a style that was meant to represent the 17th century, it is safe to assume that his fencing techniques were not one-to-one copies of what was being taught in 19th century fencing salles. He was a true romantic, vaunting and idealizing the past, while lamenting the present. He imagined, with obvious longing, how Poles in the 17th century fought with their sabers, and this is the best way to approach his work.

---

111   In the foreword of Chris Holzman's *The Art of the Dueling Sabre*, he describes how mid to late 19th century Italian saber techniques had abandoned elbow or shoulder-powered cuts in favor of the use of the wrist. Attacks delivered from the wrist lacked in power, and so the larger but stronger cuts were re-introduced by Radaelli for military purposes. They were abandoned again for push-cuts when the needs of sport fencing replaced those of military action or dueling.

"On Fencing"

by

Michał Starzewski (1801-1894)

English Translation: Daria Izdebska

The carrion crows are cawing, the startled crane took flight,

And on the Black and Podolian trails,[112] the banners of the Khan gleam in sunlight.

Across the steppe, in fire and flame, and billows of grey smoke

Tartar hordes advance in throng – Crimea's heavy stroke.

The heathens are rampant in Podolia, in bloody whirlwind they advance,

And all the lively youth is gone – and no one shouts: Huzzah!

Where are the brave Żółkiewscy?[113] Where hymns to the Mother of God?

And where is the blade of Szczerbiec,[114] the mighty sword?

Yet bear this in mind: the wolf may lose his fangs,

but never his nature.

Fencing – What is it?

Fencing is an art, or science, with which we gain the skills to use weapons for our own defense and for the purpose of disarming our opponent. As such, fencing requires specific exercises of the body which produce agility, flexibility, the speedy and balanced back-and-forth movements, and grounding. All of these skills should underlie and accompany the defense against and attack of our opponent. Thus, the entire fencing art should rely on the nimble and agile movements of our body.

The rules of reason govern these movements and thus lead us to victory. These rules tell us how to attack and defend against enemies, so that we can always gain victory in the quickest and sur-

---

112   Both the Black Trail and the Podolian (Kuchman) Trail were military and trade routes in south-eastern borders of the Polish-Lithuanian Commonwealth. From the 16th until the 18th century the Podolyan trail was used by the Crimean and Nogai Tartars to harry Podolia (now, in the Ukraine, formerly belonging to the Commonwealth). The Black Trail was used in a similar fashion and led on to Kiev and Zbaraż, and was used for attacking Volhynia. -Translator's note-

113   An important Polish noble family, whose one of the most important representatives was Stanisław Żółkiewski (1547-1620), one of the most accomplished military commanders, and also a high ranking official. -Translator's note-

114   Szczerbiec is the coronation sword of Polish kings used from the 14th till the 18th century. -Translator's note-

est of ways. The most crucial thing is to save our own strength, so that we do not spend it all too early and give our opponent an advantage over us, but to be able to have our own advantage, which is rightly due to our fortitude, bravery, and skills.

To understand fencing in such a fashion means to depend on the development of all the strengths of our body. And if we treat this as the only rule governing our actions, then we should pay utmost attention to the following – first, the positioning of our body, and second – the type of weapon with which we face our enemy. When discussing the positioning of the body we consider the fencer himself – here, the most important elements of the movement are **attacking** and **defending** (or the **clash**). Both of these fully depend on yet another skill and we shall talk about this separately in more detail. But since the construction of the weapon demands a much shorter description, it shall be discussed first. Then I shall follow with the presentation of the main tenets of the Polish school of fencing.

About the weapon

About the weapon, its external and internal attributes, and the proper names of its parts

Our Forefathers named this most essential of weapons with which they punished the invading Tartar hordes a *kord*, from the Polish verb *karać* (which means 'to punish'). The other name, *oręże*, came from the verb *orędować*, which meant 'to defend', because our forefathers would defend not only themselves, but also other nations from the heathens, and did so from times immemorial. Our forefathers did not use the weapon only in war and to aid them in their own need, but also to defend the noble female sex to which Poland owes so many good men. There was no need to force our youths to pick up a blade and a lance and jump on a horse. The younglings who had but started their education and opened their first Latin grammar by Alvarez,[115] were ready to get straight into it – Hey! Ho! Huzzah! on the field – and in the presence of the Reverend Prefect, ho!, maybe even the *Rector Magnificus* himself, they would beat whosoever was there with their *palcaty*,[116] whether he was a humanist, or an older man[117] or even a lawyer, he would be beaten shamelessly. And when the youth exchanged their *palcat* for a *kord* no bandit would ever escape. Similarly, if – God forbid –someone would have traditions and customs in disregard! Or worse yet, dishonor the fair sex! The one who sullied the national character so, would get what was coming to him. Thus, at the crack of dawn the Marshall, right in front of the earth-walls surrounding the stronghold of either the Castellan[118] or the Voivode,[119] would let the young boys fight each other with sabers, or with lances, if they had their mail on. This is how the saying was born:

---

115   A 16th century Jesuit whose grammar book was widely used. Poles learned Latin in the 17th century, whereas in the West it was abandoned in favor of vernacular languages. -Translator's note-
116   Wooden sticks or dowels used for saber practice. -Translator's note-
117   Literally, "a man with a moustache". -Translator's note-
118   Mayor of a town, city, or estate.
119   A warlord or governor.

Think virtuously – speak kindly,
be steady – beat heartily,
Be harsh on yourself – but good to another,
And you shall win the world over.
Our Ancestors were known to do so
thus: listen now and follow.

They were trained to use polearms and blades of various kinds tremendously well. They had straight blades and curved *karabele*,[120] damascenes, serpentines, *glewigi*, Teutonic, English and Swedish blades. In Poland, at national celebrations, the nobles would carry at their belts *karabels* or damascenes (*demeszki*). Military campaigns were fought with straight or curved weapons. An armored soldier or quarter armies[121] would use only a straight blade. *Bravely they cut and gave others hell – this you, yourselves know very well!*

At various diets [*sejmik*] you could see a wide variety of blades: both curved and straight, *smyczki* and *scyzoryki*, *kordy* and *oręże*, *serpentyny* and *stambułki* (made in Istanbul), *tasaki* and *brzytewki* – all these were forever busy.[122] But today we can no longer see faces and foreheads marked with the 11th article which used to shine brightly over the drooping eye.[123] Today, the cheek is soft and smooth like a newborn's behind, with a beauty spot under the eye and a blush that is painted on. A face that can fence with words – but not with a blade.

In quarrels of which the fair sex was the cause, or when defending his honor, or avenging offence – the Italian would sneakily use his dagger, the Frenchman openly attack with a smallsword, and the Swede or the German, or some other foreigner, would thrust with his straight blade. The Pole, however, would use his saber-armed hand on the head and the nose and the ears of his opponent, so that the arrogant lout would always carry a memento and a lesson on how to behave properly. This is why the Sarmatian despised the dagger, the smallsword appeared only for a while during the modern era and the reign of the Wettin dynasty, and even then only at court – and the straight blade came to us from Germany.[124] But there was only one faithful *karabela*, which defended one's life and taught a lesson to all impudent men, and reminded that the face is there not just to look pretty, but to face up to the opponent with a weapon in hand.

But today, when we're losing the balance between developing the attributes of the mind and the body, and when we see the entire life of our forefathers in glimpses only, let the art itself take place of the constant exercising of the blade, because it still engages the natural quickness of the heart and will help to develop and polish the gemstone that is already inside us.

---

120   A *karabela*, a type of saber.
121   *Wojska kwarciane* was the regular army in the Commonwealth, named so after the tax amount (fourth, that is quarter) that was devoted to its up keeping. -Translator's note-
122   All are types of swords.
123   Presumably, this refers to the scars made by the tip of the saber on the cheek that could resemble the sign for an article of law: § 11. -Translator's note-
124   He is referring to Augustus the Strong.

The fencing art requires, above all, the knowledge of various blades, and in today's battles there are only two types of them: curved and straight. The curved ones (illustration 1), that is those which are in an arced shape, which we call sabers (*szable*) today; and the straight ones (illustration 2), which are called *pałasz*, from Hungarian. To follow in the footsteps of our fathers we shall call the first one *kord*, and the second one *oręż*. Both will be called cutting weapons.

In the olden days no nobleman would buy a *kord* without testing it first. When he tested it, he gracefully tapped the pommel – then drew the saber – he peered closely, but before he would take a closer look, he would usually wipe it clean with the flap of his outer garment (*kontusz*). He knew of a trick that the traders were using: that is to smear some fat over the blade to hide any imperfections which would have easily gone unnoticed if it were a German who was attempting to buy a blade.

Then he looked upon the surface of the blade and if he saw his face reflected there, he knew that the workmanship was good and the steel tempered properly.

By running his thumb along the **spine** of the blade he could feel all the nicks and chips there. He would also run a piece of flint from the crossguard to the point along the spine so that the weapon sent out showers of sparks. He followed this with a cross cut in the air, and when the sound was equal on both sides, he said to himself: "That is well tempered steel!"[125]

Then he looked down the spine of the *kord*, placing it next to his right eye to see the curvature; he twirled his moustache, looked at the flat of his blade and read engraved there: PRO GLORIA ET PATRIA! [*For Glory and Homeland!*], and the second one: PRO FIDE, LEGE ET REGE [*For Faith, Law and King*]; and from the period of the Wettin dynasty, the famous name AR [*Augustus Rex*]. Then he knew full well, without any doubt, that this was an *Augustówka* [a saber from the time of King Augustus]. Sometimes a quotation from the Al-Koran was inscribed on the blade – then he knew that the saber belonged to someone who is now in the kingdom of heaven. Then he would smack the saber gently on the blade, making it ring – a certain distance from the cross – and then holding it nonchalantly, as if he was weighing it on his finger, he would ask about the price.

"Pay whatever you think it's worth!" was often the answer.
"Oh, wait a minute, Sir!" The nobleman responded. "Is it as good as it looks?"
"You are free to try it out, noble Sir, especially since it is already in your hand."

And here the testing began: cutting backwards, hitting the surface of the water with the flat of the blade, or – more often – hitting the pommel of the saddle with the flat. Then the blade would thunk, tremble, ring, and it would either shatter or gleam in its core. And then once again he would measure it up to his right eye, and slowly put it on the scales of the saber-smith and weigh it against ringed gold.

"Better than gold, that's how good it is!" he would mutter under his breath.

And then it would hang at his belt, and his eye would gleam like an eagle's eye, and no one could stand up to him.

---

125   The cross cut is a feature often mentioned, but not clearly described, in Polish sources.

With a proud cheek and a sure step
It is Mars who guides your gaze!

And verily the true damascene blades were worth their weight in gold. Those who were richer than kings and khans and shahs and sultans would receive them as gifts. Quite often, the godfather would give a damascene blade to his godson. And those were certainly the times to do so. Thus: the German blades were taken at Hundsfeld[126] in the reign of King Bolesław III Wrymouth; Persian and Circassian [Adyghe] swords were taken at Kiev in the reign of King Bolesław the Bold; Lithuania gave us Tartar sabers when Witold reigned; we received Teutonic swords when Jagiełło was King; the Baghdad damascenes were delivered from Palestine; and the true Turkish blades had to be brought by Jan III himself from the Battle of Vienna.[127] Cossacks would also sail to Istanbul in their *czajka* boats to get them. This is where we end our account of the virtues of various blades.

An experienced old dog feels the grip of his saber in his hand and knows how to spin it well, with skill and power. When you look at him, it seems as if the blade was lighter than a feather, it shimmers like a colorful rainbow; and suddenly, like a lighting strike, it hits the opponent.

1

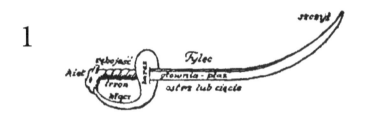

The *waga* [vah-gah] of the blade was known and valued everywhere and everyone knew how to use it. The *waga* of the blade! It is no small matter, Sir! Let us look at it in detail!

2

The *waga* of the blade – What it is and what principles it follows, and also how to choose a good blade for your own hand[128]

3

Before we find out what the *waga* of the blade is, we must first look at one very natural line of reasoning. Thus:

---

126   Battle of Psie Pole, 1109. -Translator's note-

127   Jan III Sobieski, the Battle of Vienna, 1683. -Translator's note-

128   A note of explanation: Starzewski differentiates between three concepts: *ciężar*, *waga*, and *podajność*. Literally, in Polish both *ciężar* and *waga* can mean simply 'weight', but waga has the additional connotations of 'balance' (as in: *waga* 'scales'), whilst *ciężar* is usually involved with gravity. *Podajność* does not appear in the main Polish dictionaries I found at all. I feel there are no exact equivalents in English that are good for rendering these three, and any fixed choice might impose a particular interpretation on the text that may not necessarily be correct. In my understanding, *ciężar* is the weapon's own weight, as one of the forces that counterbalance the strength of the hand. *Podajność* seems like a quality of the blade to be differently influenced by different forces – if pressed at the weak, the blade will move easily, if pressed at the strong, it will not budge. *Waga* on the other hand is the actual mechanic behavior of the blade, particularly its balance with regard to the forces operating on it and the forces with which it operates. I did not choose to translate *waga* as 'balance', because there's also the Polish word *równowaga*, which is used to denote balance and is used as such by Starzewski. -Translator's note-

Before you engage in a fight, remember that the blade of the weapon is nothing else and cannot be anything else but the extension of your own arm, and conversely: your shoulder, from the armpit right to the hand, is nothing but at a long grip of the saber. From this emerge several important truths to the fencer:

1. The movements of the arm to the left and to the right are directed by the armpit, and more importantly:

2. The arm should forget about bending in the elbow almost completely, and all the cuts:

3. Should be performed through the movements of the hand only.[129]

Taking this as our most inviolable principle we conclude that: the mobility of the hand and the rigidity of the arm, that is the **strength of the hand** and **the extension of the arm**,[130] are the first and necessary conditions of our fencing art.

We should call the entire extended arm of the fencer from the armpit until the tip of the blade the fencer's **striking.** This Striking is a lever, which is a class three bar, according to the laws of mechanics by Archimedes, and thus it should follow almost exactly the same laws. So: the fulcrum is at the shoulder, the effort in the middle, and the resistance – that is the heart of the cut – at the tip of the blade. Here, the most important thing is to find the balance, and know where to stop the tip of the blade – at all times and from all places – at the centre of all the converging core cuts. This centre happens to be in the middle of a man's chest, (see illustration 5) and is called **the core**, and from this, it follows that all the cuts can be divided into two main types: **the cuts to the hand** and **the cuts to the core**. The former are **short**, because they reach just to your opponent's hand, the latter are **deep**, as they strike at the opponent's face, chest, arms, and we shall discuss these later on.

Bearing that in mind, it is easy to understand that the *ciężar* **of the blade** as outlined above, – should correspond to the **strength of the hand**, and conversely, the strength of the hand should correspond to the *ciężar* of the blade. The right *ciężar* of the blade is found thusly:

In the distance of five inches at most, counting from the base of the crossguard, put the given blade on your index finger and weigh it. If the blade balances well against the hilt, the saber will be appropriate for your own strength and you will not go past the core of cuts with those cuts which you perform with it. But this is still what we call *podajność* of the weapon, not yet it's *waga*.

We can distinguish two types of *podajność* – the **cutting** and the **defending**. The surest way to reach the opponent is with the tip of the blade – you defend from his cuts by intercepting them or guiding them aside with the length of the blade itself, particularly with the strong of the blade. Thus the **cutting** *podajność* starts at the tip and goes towards the crossguard – the **defending** *podajność* goes from the crossguard towards the tip. And the point of equality of them both is located in the middle of the blade, where the cut is equal to the parry or defense, and the parry or defense is equal to the cut. Starting from this point, the closer you strike to the **strong**, the weaker your cut will be – the closer you cut to the **tip,** the stronger your cut will be and the defense of your opponent the weaker, and it often goes so far that at the very tip of your opponent's blade the defense is almost zero. And even if he is defending himself in a guard, you can cut through that guard quite easily and reach him.

---

129   His advice is in line with those like Parise, whose ideas didn't hold up to military rigor and were replaced by Radaelli's more powerful cuts during the 19th century.

130   The word means literally 'keeping it strong and powerful whilst extended'. -Translator's note-

From that middle point of the blade go the two counterpointing *wagas*: the cutting and the defending. The cutting one cuts best at the weak of the blade – and the defending is strongest right at the crossguard. From those counter points to the middle, both the defense and the cutting are getting weaker closer to the middle, and that which we call the true *waga* of the blade gets weaker also – and every fencer should know it well.

To know the *waga* of the blade is to know the two opposing characteristics of its ends, and the middle of the blade is the fundamental point of this *waga*, as if the fixed point on which the two arms of the blade weigh against each other in both ways. And this is why we call it *waga*.

This *waga* results from the rules of mechanics. To keep these properties in balance and to never be pushed out of the core of the cuts, the blade, as we have shown previously, when measured 5 inches from the crossguard, should balance out the pommel. Once you understand this *waga*, then you can choose a saber that will be suited to your hand. Let us now move on to the way in which the weapon should be held.

Holding the weapon – How to do it and on what conditions

In holding the weapon we should pay attention to two particular things: the **hilt** and the **hand**. As for the hilt, there are the following:

1. *Kieł* lit. 'fang' [presumably the end of the grip]
2. Grip
3. Crossguard
4. Ring, or loop, if it has one

As regards our hand and its principle parts, we should consider:

1. The wrist
2. The thumb
3. The index finger (which is called the leading finger, *digitus vector*, or the ring finger).

This finger aids the thumb in all its workings; it also leads all the cuts, and as such is called the leading finger; and because quite often it is put into the ring or loop, we can also call it the ring finger.[131]

Thus, knowing all the principal parts and names of the *kord* – I can now take it in my hand. All this I perform in a certain tempo, that is, on my command:

"Prepare for drawing! – To weapons!"

I raise my right hand gracefully in the air, and with a certain force I use it to hit the hilt, counting the beats in my mind – one! Two! I draw – Three! I place my hilt against my chest and when the point is towards my opponent face – that's the art of drawing the saber! And so:

---

131   Mind here that the index finger is called the ring finger, unlike our modern understanding of the ring finger. -Translator's note-

1. The fang of the grip is resting against the wrist of the hand and firmly pressed against the muscle of the base of the thumb.

2. The Thumb lies alongside the ridge of the grip

3. The Ring-Finger is at the right side of the grip – it can be placed in a twofold fashion – if there is no ring, then it rests at the crossguard, if there is a ring – that's where it should be placed, by the bending of the first joint of the digit. But even better in its responsiveness than a ring, is a leather loop. Because drawing it more towards the hand, I can control the movements of the blade very effectively; thus I have all the cuts I wish under my command, and my *kord* never leaves the centre of the core cuts – so I keep the core balance of the blade in check at all times. Thus, the *waga* of all cuts depends on this leading or ring finger.

About the stance
What it should be like and its principles.

After we have discussed how to draw and hold the weapon, before we move on to cutting, we must first know how to stand properly, and how to make our stance advantageous, so that we can (according to circumstances) make sure that each and every cut and movement is grounded most securely and surely, and has the right support. The first point of that support are our **feet**. So we turn to the direction and position of the feet first.

After the feet, we should look at the bending of the knees – this is granted second position; furthermore, **the torso, chest, arms and shoulders, hands, and face.**

The proper and advantageous positioning of these parts of the body that would be suitable for our attack, the lightening-like, subtle, but versatile mobility which should accompany every attack and defense, and correspond to our opponent's movements, is called – a **stance**. This stance, depending on the different positions, can be – **initial**, or **facing**, or **engaging**, or **cutting**, or **retreating**.

THE INITIAL STANCE
In this stance, the left foot has all the strength – and it is placed just so: when I have my right foot facing forward and in front of me – the left is placed in a half turn behind me, so that the left heel is away from the right heel at the distance of about eight inches.
In such a stance, the hand which holds the weapon is dropped down away from my right leg, and I pierce my opponent with a cold gaze, eying him up and down. Thus, I await the attack, or initiate it myself.

And if I do see that the opponent is engaging, I immediately go into my facing stance and thus I will face him – as our Forefathers said: "Face up, Brother!"[132]

---

132   Here, Starzewski is using a play on words. "Czołem, Panie Bracie!" literally means "With your Forehead, Brother", but it is also used as a salutation in Polish (you can say "Czołem!" to a group of people when you meet them). Additionally, it implies a certain bravery as in stawić czoła ('face something', lit. 'place your forehead in front of it'), means to face something courageously. Thus the stance is called 'czelna', which I chose to translate as 'facing' stance, because in English 'face' is used rather than 'forehead' (as in: facing danger, for instance, is behaving bravely). -Translator's note-

And from this we have:

THE FACING STANCE OR FACE UP, BROTHER!

The Facing stance in the Polish school should be as follows: do not change your initial stance at all, but go softer and lower on the legs, suck in your stomach, extend your arm and puff up your chest behind it, and raise the tempered [as in: tempered steel] tip of your *kord* so that it points at your opponent's right eye, and always keep it pointed at his eyes! And look at him from beneath the crossguard! And so: your knuckleguard will always protect your temple – the straight elbow will save you from a cut, and the moulinet[133] done in time will protect your chest.

Now you need to practice this stance, constantly because if you never leave it, and are quick and skillful enough to perform a moulinet in time – then you will not be cut. But it is not artful to simply stand facing your opponent, you need to also know how to attack – and thus, you also need to know how to engage and cut with your *kord*, and this is when the Engaging Stance comes into play:

THE ENGAGING STANCE

To explain this stance, I need to go back to the Initial Stance and strip it down to its component parts – firstly, the left foot is the immobile, fixed constant. From it you spring, if you want to jump – and it is also the spring of your movements back and forth.[134] On the unswerving surety of this foot depends the surety of all your other movements. Exercise it often, and also bend your knees and lean your body in and out, and if that foot can stay where it is supposed to – all is well, for the fencer and for the blade!

This foot shall be called the **retreating foot** and the right one, with which you step forward, shall be called the **advancing foot**, that is the front and back foot for short. Now understand this:

There are no, and should not be any fixed rules regarding the distance between the front foot and the back foot. All the German practices in this regard are nonsense! Because the length of your step is determined by God himself who has given you your natural height, the distance between the front foot and the back foot should be kept in such a fashion that your body can go both forwards and backwards with all certainty, and also sway to all the sides, so that the feet do not move at all from their positions, nor should they budge even a little.[135] That's the first condition. You also need to remember the second condition, which is: to lean forward (towards the brow), you should bend your front knee – and when you retreat, you should bend your back knee. Practice this moving back and forth continually, so that it can become graceful and agile, natural, and – above all – appropriate to your own strengths. In this way you will avoid a bizarre, theatrical stance governed by all those strict foreign rules, which often cost you a cut to the side, or to the face or head, if you do insist on keeping to it accurately. Then, and only then will you keep a stance that is natural to you, courageous, and appropriate to your height, your body and your strength, which will not only save your skin, but also allow you to attack your opponent.

Bearing this in mind, this is how you should move from the Facing Stance into the Engaging

---

133   A circular cut critical to the saber system.
134   Similar to a lunge.
135   This feature is found in German dussack material.

Stance:

When you see that your opponent has revealed a weak side – or **weakness** – then **attack** it! And this is how to do it – you take a step with your front foot, that is you put your right foot forward as if you mean to get him with the extension of your Initial Stance. Go forward so that you can always go back without losing any balance or strength – but also so that you are ready to jump forward again. Remember to keep the stability of your feet in control, and measure your step appropriately to height, intention and strength. And secondly, when you have complete control, be prepared in your spirit for these movements back and forth which are most comfortable to you, so that you can lean in and out every single time. With such preparation and agility, **quietly** and without noise – you take a step, counting **one!** in your mind, and that is what we call the Engaging Stance, and from it, like a lightning strike, follows:

<u>The Cutting Stance</u>

Now, when you are tense and ready for action, and sure that you can reach him in some way – push yourself off with your back foot suddenly – forward – with your front foot jump slightly up, but that needs to be already part of your step and should not make you lose balance! – and in this forward jump – CUT! And immediately go back into the Facing Stance. Now, there are two possible scenarios: either you have cut him, or you haven't. If you have cut him and you cover yourself in the Facing Stance – and he, a good fencer, knows what you were planning – and strikes from above with a cross-cut moulinet, so that you give back what you owe him with interest – then you should huddle, lean back, and point your blade continually at his eye and look at his face from beneath your crossguard – How does he look? Where is he lacking? – and this is <u>the Defending Stance</u>.

<u>The Retreating Stance</u>

But when, my brother, the nobleman goes at you without pause – and knows all the tricks – and keeps coming – then you should go into retreat, and so: do not move the tip of your blade away from his eye, the knuckleguard will protect your temple – and cut back at him, huddle more, go low on the knees, so that you are like the one who, looking straight at the sun, wants to see with an eagle's eye, but defends from the rays of the sun with his blade – and go back, backwards, low – this is your retreating stance.

But remember not to escape too far away with too fleet a step – only up to a point – wait up, Sir! – and here from a straight line of combat jump backward and sideways, and cut at him with the following cuts: – into his groin or belly from the right below *nyżkiem* [core cut 3], into his neck from the left [*w łęg* – core cut 6], into the shoulder [no cut given], or into his left hip *w trok* [core cut 9]. And we shall explain this to you in more detail, because for you to understand this, you must first be already quite versed in using the weapon.

About how to position yourself in a stance

When you know all these things, then you can stand properly; but you also need to understand and know both your own positioning, and your opponent's, so that you are able to **use** it properly and – conversely, so that you do not pass advantage to your opponent. For this, we need to ponder and comprehend the following components of this positioning:

Now, when you move from the initial to the facing stance, and lift your arm and hand that holds the weapon – then with this movement, you are opening the entire right side of the body to attacks, and your left side – as being opposite the one which would be attacked – is much less vulnerable. Also, you are opening your hand much more to attacks than your breast; but you would much rather lose your hand than your breast. The right side of your stance, because it holds in its hand the defense of your breast, is called the – **hand-side** – and the left one is called the **opposite-side**. The middle of the chest, because it is the core, and you care about it the most – is called the **core-side**. You already know how to hold your **hand-side** in all your stances. You also know how to hold the **core-side** – that is your head, breast, and stomach. The only thing left is, then, to discuss the **opposite-side**, and its first component is the **left** hand. Take your left hand behind your belt, over the hip, so that it doesn't impede you – or, bent, put it on your left shoulder blade, so that it doesn't appear anywhere and won't be cut. An old and experienced fencer often raises it up and bends it, but in such a fashion that the hand is away from his head, as if he was trying to balance the hand-side, which gives him a graceful pose. This depends on the habits and skills of the fencer, but the most important thing is to always place your left hand most advantageously, that is for it to be a help and not a hindrance, and maybe even an ornament.

There is not much more that could be said about the opposite-side in fencing, unless, of course, the fencer would switch his hands and hold his weapon in his left hand. And in that case, the entire stance is now different to the opponent, and also more dangerous, because it is as if the opponent had to face a completely new enemy. The switching of the hands is quite profitable and advantageous, but easier if someone already knows how to use the weapon with their right hand. This should be left up to the one who knows how to do it, with the cautionary remark that his left arm will become the **hand-side**, and the right, appropriately, will become the **opposite-side.**

Thus, fencing requires a stance and a good positioning of this stance – and if the **hand-side** defends him, so the **core-side** should be defended by the **hand-side**. Thus, there are only two sides relevant to fencing – the **hand-side** and the **core-side**. And since every fencer (and particularly in triple cuts, as you shall soon see for yourself) after he attacks the core, moves to the hand, and conversely, after attacking the hand, moves his blade to the core, thus in the whole affair, we only have two types of cuts – the **hand cuts** and the **core cuts**. Let us now explain both.

> "He rushes straight at me slashing with all his might;
> I withstood it, then having deferred, I slashed him
> across the pulses..."
> - Jan Chryzostom Pasek

About cuts - A sketch of the cuts to the hand and the cuts to the core

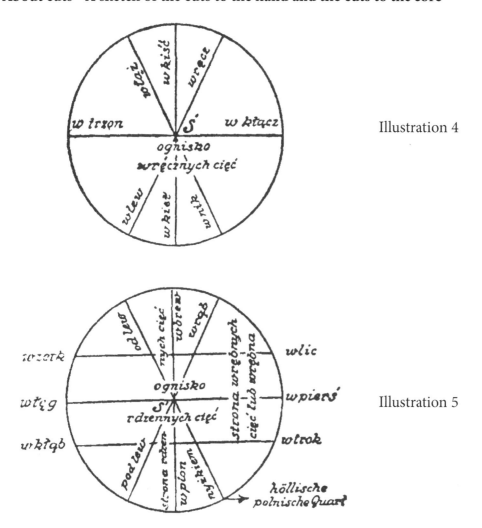

Illustration 4

Illustration 5

We can consider these cuts in two fashions; one, as to the practice [*wprawa*], and two, as to the actual fight [*rozprawa*]. In the practice, the hand-cuts should come first. It is the other way in the fight, because here the core-cuts should come first, because those are usually offensive, and what these cuts can't do, then the hand-cuts should make up for.

About Hand-cuts

Imagine a certain circle (See, image 4) of a roughly two-foot diameter. This is what we call the rim of hand cuts, and in the centre Ś[136] we place the hand that is holding the weapon. Your own hand, with the movements of the **wrist**, targets it with the first cuts so:

1. As God made your hand – raise it with the spine of the blade upwards and forward, away

---

from yourself and then bring it down with the blade into the middle of your opponent's hand, creating the line a-s, thus cutting him in the hand, and so **hand-wards.** And this first cut is thus called, **hand-wards cut.**

You need to be wary here; since you are performing this cut solely with the movement of your hand, and bringing the blade down, you cannot bring it lower than the natural characteristics of your hand will allow; so always remember to stop the blade with the natural lowering of your hand, and thus, in the centre of your opponent's hand. This centre is that 'core centre' which we discussed previously. If you, however, pass this centre, you can feel that the weight of your weapon pulls out your hand – overcomes your own strength – and after several cuts you will feel a pain in the hand that will often make it impossible for you to make further cuts. So here, you must remember the *podajność* of the weapon, which we mentioned above. And also the *waga* of the weapon – which is necessary for deep cuts – will make itself known. Make sure to pick the right weapon for your own hand, and you will not make laughing stock of yourself. And, secondly, make sure that its **weight** is appropriate for your strength, and the other way round. To sum up, your *kord* cannot ever go beyond the core centre of the cuts, e.g. aŚb, but needs to stop always and ever in the middle. And following from that:

2. You raise your blade again, but when raising it with the spine forward – you turn the blade towards the left and towards the vein in the wrist of your opponent's hand, as if you were to cut into the extension of the leading finger – so *w łąż*, and stopping the weapon in the centre again,

3. You turn up the cut downwards and away from yourself, so from left to right and you cut up into your opponent's hand – here, see how the pinky goes into the hand, so you would like to enter it also – and the third cut is thus called [*wnik*] – the **penetrating-cut.**

4. Then you once again turn your own hand, and as if you would like to cut up into the left of his hand; thus the 4th cut is called [*wlew*] –**into-left-cut**

5. Then, again, turn away your weapon and target his palm, but this is where the knuckleguard [*kłącz*] of the weapon protects him – and so this cut is called [*wkłącz*] **into-knuckleguard-cut**

6. Again, turn it – and you target the fingers that hold the grip, so the cut is called **into-grip-cut** [*wtrzon*]

7. With the next one, you attack into the wrist of the hand directly from above, and thus it's called **into-wrist-cut.** [*wkiść*] And finally:

8. You cut from below, directly opposite from the previous cut, that is into the base of the hand, where the wrist is hidden by the pommel [*kieł*] and we call this: [*wkieł*]

Thus, we have eight of the shallow, or short, or hand cuts – and they are: *Wręcz! Włąż! Wnik! Wlew! Wkłącz! Wtrzon! Wkiść! Wkieł!* Make sure to pay attention to the illustration, because they all have clear and natural names. And now, after all these hand cuts, let us now become acquainted with:

Deep Cuts, otherwise known as Core Cuts

You should perform them in much the same way as the hand cuts; the fencer's body, however, is no longer divided into three sides (hand-side, core-side, opposite-side) as in the hand cuts, but rather the sides have different names now, and that is for the following reasons:

The right side of the fencer, because it carries its own cuts, and is the most vulnerable to being cut, but it also is the one which **cuts**, should therefore, in those deep cuts, be called the **cutting side**.

The middle part – because you still protect the core of your life – will remain the **core-side**. But the left side, because to reach it you need to chop your way into it by getting through the first two sides, then it rightfully deserves the name of the 'hacking side'. From this we now know that the deep cuts can be divided into three types: cutting, core and hacking through. Let us now look at their order:

The Order of Cutting, Core and Hacking Cuts

Bearing all this in mind, imagine once again the rim of the core cuts, so a circle that is slightly larger than the circle for the hand, for which the centre Ś. (see illustration 5) is located between the armpits of the opponent and directed at the core of his chest, and once again this is the centre of all your cuts, in which every single cut should stop – and as in the hand cuts – your hand should never allow the cut to go past it. Otherwise, it is your own fault that you did not pick the right weapon for your hand. The circumference of the circle of the deep cuts covers: the arms, the shoulders, the head, the chest, up to the middle of your body, below the hips (see illustration 5).

According to these rules, this is how you should perform your cuts:

1. Raising your weapon with the spine of the blade away from yourself – just as in hand cuts – you cut your opponent into the left arm of the hacking-through side, so the 'hack', and the blade should go right unto the centre ś., into the chest, and thus this cut is called 'hack' [wręb].

2. You turn the blade towards yourself, and you make a circle from your **left** into the right, so this is **from-left** [odlew]; this is your second cut.

3. Then, you move your weapon in an opposite fashion – so you use a low cut, that is from the right and below, into the stomach – and this cut is known as **low-cut** [nyżek].

This cut has occasionally been called the Turkish cut, because we would cut the bellies of the Turks open using this cut, and during the diets [sejmik], many a nobleman would cut open the knot on the sash of the Voivode, but did not do more than that, which meant: "With respect, but cuttingly, Sir!" and then the Voivode knew who he was dealing with – and it wasn't too bad for him in those times. Sometimes, a German would come here with his own weapon – and would almost always receive as a souvenir this cut, and so, in trepidation, they named our **low-cut**: DIE HÖLLISCHE POLNISCHE QUARTE [The Hellish Polish Fourth].

4. From the low-cut, as if you were sweeping aside the lower ends of your long tunic, you circle with the weapon from under the low left, and this is as if it were a 'left low cut' – and this is

called the **under-left** [*podlew*], because you hit him from your left.

5. After those four cuts, you can hit him through his armpit into the chest – and that's **into-chest** [*wpierś*] cut.

6. And then, from the left, an opposite cut, but much like the previous one, whereupon the base of the opponent's head comes to the nook of the neck, and there you slash – **into-nook** [*wlew*]!

7. Our people cut from high up as well! So you reach the face, and ho! Maybe you can carve a mark there, whilst you're at it, marking the lordling's cheek! And so – **into-cheek** [*wlic*]!

8. And the opposite cut to that one, into the left eye, and so – **into-eye**! [*wzerk*]

9. And then again, from below, into the left hip, where you usually fasten the cords of your sheath – and so the cut is called – **into-cords**! [*wtrok*]

10. And then move again to the right hip, on the other side, and make it better with - ***wkłęb***!

Italian

ITALIAN TEXT BY NICOLETTO GIGANTI

In 2012, Giganti's second book on the rapier was rediscovered by Joshua Pendragon and Piermarco Terminiello. The book was so obscure and rare that even contemporaries of Giganti chided him for promising a second book but never delivering. The second book, dating from 1608, is a treatise covering a variety of techniques, including the cut. While the rapier is primarily a thrusting weapon, Giganti noted that most swordsmen were not skilled and would cut with it. Furthermore, when facing multiple opponents, the cut was vital: if you tried to thrust, even if successful, the blade would become stuck and in turn the other opponent would hit you. It is here that Giganti's advice lends itself to the Polish saber.

Giganti describes briefly how to use cuts to parry and respond to attacks when facing multiple opponents. While Father Jezierski does no more than use the phrase "cross-cut", Giganti spells out an interpretation. Furthermore, the concept of cross-cutting was also used in another early 17th century rapier manual by Hans Wilhelm Schöffer von Dietz, giving us two period-texts that discuss the concept with rapiers.[137]

Giganti's instructions lend themselves to the Polish saber as a simple, effective way to deal with one or more opponents by using cross-cuts.

---

137   Renier van Noort provided a translation of Wilhelm Schöffer von Dietz which spelled out cross cutting, including other options differing from Giganti, such as cutting from right to left toward the face, then cutting again, left to right, but targeting the leg. In both cases the cross is more like an x than a +.

"Libro Secundo"

[excerpt]

by

Nicoletto Giganti (Early 17th Century)

English Translation: Piermarco Terminiello and Joshua Pendragon[138]

Preface to the Reader on the Nature of Cuts

I would like to teach you how to defend yourself with cuts, in cases of necessity, against two or three people. If you are attacked by two people, as often occurs, if you cut a *mandrittto*[139] at one, in that tempo the other will strike at you. While if you thrust at one, in that tempo you will take a thrust from another. Therefore you will quickly find yourself dead, as has happened to many.

In order to both attack and defend, I want you to keep your sword high as if to deliver a *mandritto*. If both thrust at you simultaneously, you should cut a *mandritto* into their swords, followed by a *roverscio*.[140]

The *mandritto* should be delivered so it almost wounds your enemy's neck, and finishes ready to attack again from the left. In this manner the *mandritto* has two effects, it offends and protects at the same time. Having delivered the *mandritto* you should bring your body back and foot back, put the sword under your left arm ready for the *roverscio*, then quickly execute this *roverscio* as follows. It should begin by attacking your opponent's neck, and end once more on your right side.

The *mandritto* and *roverscio* therefore attack in the form of a cross.[141] With this method you both attack and defend since your sword must inevitably find your enemies' weapon. Note that these *mandrittti* and *roversci* should be delivered long, hard, quickly, and without ever stopping. As soon as you perform the *mandritto* the *roverscio* should always follow. Likewise, having delivered the *roverscio*, you should execute the *mandritto* without any delay. In other words, they should continue like a wheel.

> "I will face him - as our Forefathers said: "Face up, Brother!"
>
> - Michał Starzewski

---

138   Joshua Pendragon and Piermarco Terminiello, *The Lost Second Book of Nicoletto Giganti*, (London: Vulpes, 2013), 47-48.

139   A right-to-left descending cut.

140   A left-to-right descending cut.

141   The word "cross" could mean something shaped like a + or an x. In this case, it is an x shape.

Italian Text by Antonio Marcelli

In 1686, Antonio Marcelli published "The Rules of Fencing" in which he laid out his notions of the use of the rapier, including a more reserved (but easier to recover from) lunge. His rules included four books, and the fourth book described the use of the saber against the rapier (which was named simply "the sword") and the rapier against the saber.

There is no clear indication if the saber described by Marcelli is a Polish saber, though he does note that Poles used such weapons. Marcelli uses the word *sciabla*, which bears similarity to the word *szabla*, the Polish term for the saber. Researcher Carlo Parisi surmises that Poland's rescue of Vienna in 1683 and its wars against the Ottomans may have spread Polish military culture to Italy, hence the use of the word *sciabla* and Marcelli's comments that the weapon was old but new to Italy, and just recently made available.

The manual refers to the saber only in the context of the rapier, and the artwork provided does not clearly match up to what might be regarded as Polish sabers. Thus, there are hints at the use of the Polish saber, but only in a limited capacity.

Some of the key advice provided by Marcelli is that the saber, when opposing the rapier, should be used with wrist-cuts only, to prevent a rapier fencer from finding a large tempo opening in which to thrust. Marcelli noted that the saber should be used with numerous quick cuts, both offensive and defensive. He believed that the saber could not be used as a thrusting weapon, and furthermore warned his readers to not attempt many of the techniques he wrote about earlier in his treatise since they applied only to the rapier.

"About the Rules of Fencing"
4th Book

[excerpts]

by

Antonio Marcelli (Late 17th Century)

English Translation: Carlo Parisi[142]

How to use the saber against the sword and how to defend yourself with the sword against the saber

I don't know why I've never read anything about saber fencing in manuals, modern or ancient, but I know for sure that this is an ancient weapon that is used in many nations, especially the eastern ones, such as Sweden, Poland, Hungary and Turkey, and many other places different from Italy for climate, religion and rituals.

I think that, being all fencing manuals written by Italian authors, they (the authors) just wrote about what you can buy and use in Italy. They just wrote about the rapier, because it is the only weapon in our tradition and the only one allowed by the princes.

Today, I notice wearing a saber has become an habit for some people, not a few of them trust to use it in various cases, therefore I decided not to neglect this weapon.

Below, I'm giving you some instructions about saber play.

The way to grip the saber and how many parts it is divided in

The saber is a single edged weapon, three palms long, a more or less. It is not straight like the sword, but somewhat curved at the point, where it becomes double edged and the blade assumes a tongue shape.

The blade is at least four times broader than the rapier's, because of this, of its considerable weight, and the edge, which is very acute, the saber cuts vigorously and strongly. This weapon is very dangerous because of its cuts, that are much more lethal than the rapier's and they can chop off limbs cleanly sometimes.

The saber's blade is not divided in three parts like the rapier's: *forte*, *terzo* and *debole*, it is considered to be made of just one part, because the whole blade has the same strength and quality at all points.[143] The saber is considered to be all *forte*, because you can hurt and defend with any part of its blade, close to the point, to the hilt, or in the middle, between the two. You can wound the

---

142   Carlo Parisi provided both images and the translation; the original work can be found in the digital Raymond J. Lord Collection. http://www.umass.edu/renaissance/lord/collection.html.
143   *Forte* is the back of the blade, *terzo* is the middle, and *debole* is the tip.

enemy with any part of a saber's edge (I say "edge", because you do not thrust with a saber), all parts are just as strong, because the blade is all the same.

The saber is to be held in a "locked key" fashion, by inserting the index finger in that hollow which is found in its cross,[144] so that the grip is fast and secure, able to resist violent action, and one doesn't lose the grip on it, which could easily happen, if one held it in another way, or tried to play with it like he was using a rapier.

Here some arguments are not valid, those I stated about the sword don't hold, we're talking about a totally different weapon, in nature and play, it is, anyway, necessary to practice its play, despite different in rules, in order to find rules appropriate to the instrument (the saber), with which they are supposed to be used.[145]

Guard and parries with the saber

The guard of the saber doesn't imply the same stance I taught for the rapier. Your stance will be with the body straight upright; when you play with the saber you have to keep your torso up, and not bend forward, and the feet well planted on the ground, so you don't risk to lean into the cuts, because, most of the time, cuts miss their target and could unbalance you in the recovery phase, when they meet no resistance.

To defend yourself from the thrusts of the rapier, you will use the usual cuts and techniques of the saber, cuts, delivered in a quick succession, will both defend and offend.

However, we must say that, in order to get the desired effect, you must use the saber swiftly, so that the cuts are many, quick and close together, the path of your cuts should be almost impossible to see. If your saber play is slow, your opponent will find the time and the place for a thrust.

You will also have to adapt to the measure your opponent sets and get the openings he gives you.

It is possible to advance and retreat using short and solid steps, one should not make long steps and overreach.

It happens that your opponent doesn't dare coming in distance to strike, but throws strikes from out of distance to keep you at bay. In such a case, you can parry, stepping in the same time, in order to get closer to the opponent and hit him with a cutting riposte.

All the cuts explained in the first part of the book can be used with the saber, the main ones being the *mandritto* and the *riverso* either *fendenti* or *obliqui*, because they are the most dangerous, since they hit high, in the head area.[146] Although all saber cuts are effective, these give you a better chance to quickly overcome the opponent.

---

144   Maybe it's a finger ring, in this case, this would suggest an Italian *Storta* is the weapon Marcelli writes about.

-Translator's note-

145   He uses the word 'sword' in reference to the rapier as described in his prior books.

146   A *mandritto* is an inside cut, a *riverso* an outside, a *fendete* is vertical while an *oblique* is angled. -Translator's note-

How to use feints with the saber

You can use feints in saber play, although it's not so easy, by pretending to cut a target and cutting another instead. One way to feint, from which the others can be deduced, can be seen in the following picture.

147

> "Our people cut from high up as well! So you reach the face, and ho! Maybe you can carve a mark there, whilst you're at it, marking the lordling's cheek!"
> - Michał Starzewski

---

147   The hat may be a *kolpak*, a Polish, fur cap often decorated with a feather. The facial hair is more akin to the Middle East.

The attacker feints a *mandritto tondo*[148] to the hip, the defender tries to parry it, not being able to slip it, opposing the forte of the sword, however, since the attacker does not commit to that cut, the defender gets hit, in the same time, in the head by a *riverso*.

In order to have the necessary speed, for such feints, one must remember the universal rule regarding cuts: they are to be delivered with the wrist only, without moving the whole arm, or they become wide and slow movements.

You can feint a *mandritto tondo* and hit with the *riverso*, or you can feint a *riverso* and hit with a *mandritto*, which would be the situation represented in the picture, if the attacking knight, feinting on the line A, compelling the defender to parry, in the same time recovered the sword along the line C and cut on the line B. All the other ways to feint follow from this one and one can learn them, by practicing long enough, understanding which occasions give him a chance to use feints to his advantage.

How to get to wrestling with the saber

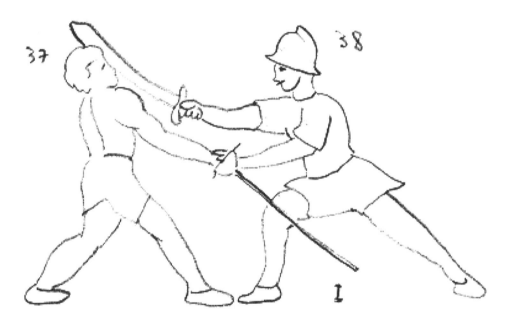

One of the advantages coming from using the saber against the rapier is that the one who has the saber can come to grips, but the other can't.

As I said: grips can follow many actions. In the previous picture, the knight 38 has performed an inside parry, then, lunging in, and using his opponent's effort to deliver his strike, he took the grip in the way shown.

---

148   Inside, horizontal cut. -Translator's note-

The knight who got hit could not escape this quick action because, being his position one of disadvantage, his disengage was by necessity slower than his assailant's attack.

Which actions aren't to be performed with the saber against the sword

The actions to be performed with the saber are the ones I previously explained, one has to avoid the infinite set of actions that belong to rapier fencing, because they are good with the rapier, but dangerous with the saber.

Single time actions, which are so important with the rapier, are very dangerous with the saber, because it is a cutting weapon and cannot hit the opponent with the edge and set aside his blade at the same time: offence doesn't defend at the same time, so you cannot offend in single time.

With the saber, you don't perform the *quarte*, the *sottobotte*, the *passate* and the *fianconate*, or the others I taught for the rapier.[149] We are in a totally different context and we have to use the techniques that cope with the instrument we're using.

Perfection in saber play comes from a long and conscious practice, that makes the arm strong and nimble, developing the speed and readiness that are necessary. Such virtues have to be developed to the point that you can close any possible way on the enemy's thrusts, by way of cutting in quick series.

Pay attention to measure: don't bring your body close to the opponent's point, because his thrust has twice the reach of your cut: not just because of the nature of the cut, which has a shorter range than the thrust, not being given upon a stretched arm and a forward bent torso, but also for the short reach of the saber, that has a shorter blade than the rapier.

One has to be very cautious in striking in single time, with the saber, and it is more advisable to do so in double time, especially when you see that you've set aside the opponent's point and you can close and cut without being hit by his thrust.

It follows, from what we said, that one that acts upon appropriate rules, acts safely.

Footwork must support the cut, giving it more power and strength, but it must always be fit to the natural movement of the strike. You can step forward and backward, to the left or to the right, but always making short steps, keeping the torso upright and well centred between the feet.

Keep your balance and walk without haste. Footwork has to match the action one is performing. One has to be strong and stable on the ground, with the body on a line and well gathered, so that he doesn't become unstable and fall, for the fury of the cuts.

The arm often gets tired and weak, because of the weight of the saber, the strength of the cuts and the length of the fight. In this case, being smart, you can catch breath and rest, without letting the opponent notice you are tired because, if the opponent noticed that you're exhausted, he could press upon you with his thrusts, while your cuts are slow. You can break measure, and get farther away from the enemy, by being smart and pretending to assume a better position or to be planning some action, so that your enemy doesn't pursue you with his thrusts; this will al-

---

149   These are all single-time counters with the rapier. -Translator's note-

low you to rest and come back to the fight stronger. It is necessary, though, to pretend that your slower moves and retreat depend upon your intention to cheat the opponent and not upon the necessity to recover.

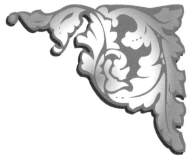

"A nobleman buckled on a saber whenever he would leave the house, and took a horseman's war-hammer in his hand."

- Jedrzej Kitowicz

German

German Text by Paulus Hector Mair, Joachim Meyer and Jacob Sutor

In the German tradition of martial arts, the dussack was a training tool and later a sportive weapon. The dussack was made of wood or leather, and bore similarities to a saber in that it offered only limited hand protection, it was curved, and it was designed to cut rather than thrust.[150]

Paulus Hector Mair produced an expensive and voluminous book on the fencing arts of the 16th century.[151] Within his *Opus Amplissimum de Arte Athletica* were full-color plates depicting the use of the dussack. German and Polish interaction was common during the 15th and 16th centuries, and the concepts of the dussack can apply to the use of the Polish saber.[152]

A German contemporary of Mair was Joachim Meyer who operated a fencing school in Strasbourg. Meyer created several treatises, including one dedicated to Otto von Solms,[153] in which Meyer referred to the dussack as the basis for all cutting weapons. In one illustration, a Pole, complete in *żupan* and sporting a distinctive Polish style of moustache, wields a dussack. The connection to Poland is clear, and so the ideas for how to use both the dussack and the Polish saber had at least some level of interaction in the 16th century. A later edition of Meyer's work from 1570, dedicated to Johann Casimir and entitled *Gründtliche Beschreibung der Kunst des Fechtens*, describes the cross-cut, a technique referenced but not explained by Father Jezierski. Jacob Sutor's manual, *Neues Künstliches Fechtbuch*, was reprinted in 1612, with its original date currently unknown. The Sutor manual is possibly an outright copy of Meyer, or more generously, an updated version of his work that includes different artwork and descriptions.[154]

150   The nature of a dussack is expanded upon here: HROARR http://www.hroarr.com/the-dussack/
151   Mair ultimately paid with his life for the book. Its cost (as well as other personal excesses) led to his hanging when the city officials discovered he had been embezzling from the city treasury. An image of the sad event can be found here - http://www.fioredeiliberi.org/phpBB3/download/file.php?id=1075
152   Wiktenauer, http://wiktenauer.com/wiki/Mair accessed 6-19-2013.
153   HROARR, http://www.hroarr.com/the-history-of-joachim-meyers-treatise-to-von-solms/accessed 6-21-2013.
154   Wiktenauer, http://wiktenauer.com/wiki/Jakob_Sutor_von_Baden accessed 1-31-2014.

Opus Amplissimum de Arte Athletica

[Image Sample]

Compiled by Paulus Hector Mair (1517-1579)

Two examples of dussack plates compiled by Mair.[155] The ability to lean toward and away from an opponent is a feature of fencing with both dussack and Polish saber, and correlates with Starzewski's description.

---

155   Copy of Mair dussack plates by Mariana López-Rodríguez.

Opus Amplissimum de Arte Athletica

[excerpts]

Compiled by Paulus Hector Mair (1517-1579)

English Translation: Keith P. Myers

This play describes the use of the *creizhau* or cross cut after displacing an incoming attack.[156]

When you come together at the closing, it happens with these positions: your right foot is set forward, your Dussack is held with the hilt near your right knee with your left hand behind near the point (left side of illustration). He then strikes to your opening from above, so go up with your Dussack above your head such that your left foot is set forward. Thus his strike is displaced. Then immediately strike with a doubled Cross Cut to his head.

If he strikes you double like this from above and you have your Dussack at your right leg with the long edge directed at your opponent, the point directed at the ground, and your right foot set forward (right side of illustration), shove this away crosswise with your short edge. Then immediately set upon him with a cut from below on his right arm and grab his right elbow with your left hand so that you shove him from you. Follow outward with your left leg and strike him to the upper opening.

If he shoves you from himself like this and intends to strike you from above, spring backwards with your left foot so that you can once again come to your work.

When you come to close with the opponent, the Schaitelhaw (Vertex Strike) happens like this: stand with your right foot forward and strike with an extended arm to his head.[157]

---

156   Copy of Meyer dussack plates by Ksenia Kozhevnikova.
157   Copy of Meyer dussack plates by Ksenia Kozhevnikova.

If you strike straight at you from above like this and you stand with your left foot forward, strike a similar one and while striking grab his right hand with your left. Thus you catch him and can send the Schaitelhaw to his head (as in illustration).

If he has caught you like this and thrown the Schaitelhaw, step with your left foot in front of his right and grab his right with your left forward near the Dussack so that you can cut through to the face.

If he intends to cut through to your face like this, step back with your left foot and turn yourself up with your Dussack at your right side such that the long edge stands above. Then immediately strike quickly to his left side. If he displaces this, spring with your right foot to his right side and strike with a doubled Creizhaw (Cross-Cut) to his head.

> "Also, you are opening your hand much more to attacks than your breast; but you would much rather lose your hand than your breast."
> - Michal Starzewski

Meyer's Treatise Dedicated to Otto von Solms[158]

[excerpts]

by Joachim Meyer (1537-1571)

English Translation: Kevin Maurer

The fencer on the right wears a żupan, has a moustache,[159] wears Polish-style boots and sash, and wears a coat called a *ferezeya*.[160] Meyer must have had either a Polish student or teacher on-hand to be a model for the drawing. Interaction between the Commonwealth and German lands was common, with Poland importing many German notions and eventually even a German king! The royal army in particular was modeled along German/Western lines.

A sample of Meyer's dussack techniques that reference the cross cut are as follows:

Quick Cut[161]

Mark thus when you stand before one in the Bow, and he will not cut so pull upwards into the Watch as if you would cut from high especially if he does nothing, wind in the air and cut with the long edge from under to his right arm quickly and jerk the Dussack again around to your left

---

158   MS A.4º.2
159   In Poland it was customary to have a shaved head and long mustache. In Western Europe beards were popular.
160   Copy of Meyer dussack plates by Ksenia Kozhevnikova..
161   Keith P. Myers notes that Meyer divides attacks into *schiessen* (cuts) and *hauen* (hacks). The cross cut is of the *hauen* variety.

shoulder, from there cut a defense strike through his right, to the arm or above the arm through to his face, and then cut a Cross or a Driving cut.

Swinger

The first is a taking out from your left and a winding out with the Flat, the other is a Strong cut from your left through his face with the Long edge with a two-fold strike through the Cross.

An Example of a Cut

Stand with your left foot forward and hold your dusack in the Steer.

162

Step and cut straight from the down through the vertical line, as far as the Midpoint where the lines cross over each other; thus you stand with your arm extended in the Longpoint.

163

This Part: From there, let the foible of your dusack drop and run off toward your left, and at the same time as your foible drops, pull your hilt up with hanging blade around your head for a stroke; mean while as you pull up your dusack for another cut, then at the same time also pull your rear foot up to the forward right one, so that you have another full step forward with your right foot to go with the cut you have prepared.[164]

---

162   Copy of Meyer dussack plates by Ksenia Kozhevnikova.
163   Copy of Meyer dussack plates by Ksenia Kozhevnikova.
164   Images courtesy Kevin Mauer translation by Jeffery Forgeng.

Meyer's Treatise Dedicated to Johann Casimir
Gründtliche Beschreibung der Kunst des Fechtens[165]

[excerpts]

by

Joachim Meyer (1537-1571)

English Translation: Jeffery L. Forgeng

The cross cut from the 1560 Meyer is further defined in the 1570 treatise.

Cross Cut

The Cross Cuts are essentially two Wrath Cuts[166] from both sides; they are executed through the two downward angling lines that run through the opponent diagonally from both sides, and cross over one another. Deliver it thus:

Stand with your right foot forward, and cut the first from your right through his left, the second from your left through his right, both diagonally through his face. Learn to do this one cut to four, five, or six, forward and back, but such that you always keep your right foot forward; therefore when you wish to step, gather your rear foot forward, so that you can step forward with the right foot; for you shall always have at least one step for both cuts that are delivered from both sides through the Cross.

You shall learn to deliver this Cross Cut, along with the aforementioned four cuts, in a fluid motion, powerfully and quickly with extended arm, and when you are cutting, to avoid holding your arm 'in the bosom' (as they say), i.e. not fully extended from you; for he who fights short and holds his arms near him is easy to deceive and hit, although the stretching out must also have its moderation and limit according to the situation of the moment.[167]

---

165 Ms. Var. 82

166 A powerful diagonal cut from above aimed at the opponent's face.

167 Jeffrey Forgeng, *The Art of Combat: A German Martial Arts Treatise of 1570*, (Palgrave MacMillan, 2006), 132.

Neues Künstliches Fechtbuch

[Excerpts]

by

Jacob Sutor (17th century)

English Translation: Keith P. Myers[168]

Sutor's manual also includes sequences that involve the cross cut, a technique known as the *kreuzhau*.

When your counterpart is not striking at you, then fence out of the Mittelhut against him thusly: note whether you can reach him, then strike with a cross cut through his face. But if he has his Dussack extended to parry, then strike with the cross cut to the hand. If he instead leads out with the Dussack, then you drive through him with the same cross cut. If he also strikes like this (with a cross cut), then quickly strike with two Mittelhau's powerfully from both sides through either of his flying strikes. With that you weaken his strikes and make his arm tired.[169] Thus you can finish him with another "after" strike to an opening.

---

168   Keith P. Myers provided both images and the translation.
169   This is similar to Giganti's technique, using cuts to deflect attacks.

Stand in the Gerade Versazung (straight parrying) or the Schnitt with the right foot forward and hold your Dussack forward with an extended arm such that the long edge is directed towards the opponent and the forward point stands out before him. From here parry his Oberhau with the long edge and thrust as soon as the Dussacks come together. Then pull your weapon completely upwards to your left such that you come into the left Stier and from there throw either an Underhau or a Mittelhau, or also diagonally over his right arm to his right through his face strong and long away from you. Forthwith strike further with cross cuts, long through his face.

German Text by Sebastian Heussler

(1581-1630/45)

The Italians spread the use of the rapier throughout Europe, and foreigners who learned the weapon later became masters of it in their own right. Sebastian Heussler was a German rapier master who published the *New Kůnstlich Fechtbuch*[170] in 1615. The work was reproduced five times and was based on the teachings of Salvator Fabris and Ridolfo Capo Ferro.[171] At the end of the first section of his manual there are three unique plates.

The three plates depict the use of sabers and not rapiers. These sabers are not deeply curved, but in one illustration the saber is in the hands of a man in Polish or Hungarian attire, whose adversary wears Turkish dress. Each plate describes a basic cutting concept, and in one case the plate's description does not match the imagery. Why Heussler added these images is unknown and nowhere else do sabers appear in the manual.[172]

Was Heussler trying to emphasize the concept of cutting by depicting sabers instead of rapiers? Was his depiction of a Pole and a Turk meant to emphasize the idea of cutting, since both cultures were known to use cutting weapons? Were Heussler's cutting techniques Polish or Eastern in origin? Did he intend the techniques to be used with the rapier, or are they three saber-specific plates, or both?

There is nothing to go on beyond the plates and the text provided.

170   The title is "New Illustrated Fencing Manual" and the same title as the Sutor work, but spelled differently.
171   Wiktenauer, http://wiktenauer.com/wiki/Sebastian_Heu%C3%9Fler, accessed 1-1-2013.
172   According to Michael Chidester, the manuscript is more curious because it borrows from a 1612 translation of Cavalcabo and also has redrawn images from Capo Ferro and Fabris. It wouldn't be surprising if the saber images came or were influenced from elsewhere. *author's note*

New Kůnstlich Fechtbuch

[excerpts]

by

Sebastian Heussler (1581-1630/45)

English Translation: Kevin Maurer[173]

Follow now how you shall cut to his right arm

If one cuts in at you, inside (of your blade) and he will also cut inside to your head, thus pay careful attention to those of his incoming cuts, that you step back with your left foot, and best him in the Measure, and also sink well backwards with your upper body, and cut simultaneous with him inside to his right arm, how you see in this following image: (Above)[174]

---

173   Kevin Maurer provided both images and the translation.
174   Heussler uses the word *"senck"* which could also mean slant backwards, or sink. -Translator's note-

From another Art

If one cuts in at you but outside your blade, to your head also, thus pay careful attention that you step well back with your left foot, from his cuts, and cut simultaneously with him outside to his right arm, how you see in the following image: (Above)[175]

When you cut in to him, to the inside of the half strong (halbe stercke) of his blade, and as soon as he will cut after to your outside, then also step back with your left foot, and cut him outside to his right arm, how you have seen on the previous image.

"The black saber was always carried by all manner of brawlers, night-prowlers and troublemakers, who found their fun in cutting people or leaving saber marks on the faces of some foppish youths, or even chasing a German in white stockings right through mud."
— Jędrzej Kitowicz

175   The figure on the right appears to be Heussler. -Translator's note-

Follow now how you should cut one to his face

If when you cut in to him, inside his blade, and he would quickly cut after you to the outside, thus step with your right foot well into him, and displace his strike nearly with the strong of your blade, as soon as his strike touches on your blade, then with your left hand under your right arm, grab away his right arm, quickly cut just then the Quarta from your left side, and from the outside to his right jaw (cheek) how in this image it is seen. (Above)[176]

> "Most often, they would cut their faces, shamefully disfiguring the handsome men, their noses and cheeks cut through, the ears cut off."
>
> - Jędrzej Kitowicz discussing the Crown Foot Guard

---

176   The text does not correlate with the image. The text seems to indicate a technique seen in multiple systems such as German messer and Spanish rapier. The sword is used to deflect a blow in the form of a hanging parry. The left hand extends under the parry to grab the opponent's (right) sword-arm. From there they can be cut. Usually a passing step is needed, but Heussler indicates it can be done with simply an extension of the lead foot. This is similar to the coming to grips that Marcelli depicts with the saber, though he uses a beat on the inside that forces the opponent's sword to the ground followed by a lunge, rather than a hanging parry on the outside.

German Text by Erhardus Henning

(1658)

Henning's text, *Kurtze Jedoch Gründliche Unterrichtung vom Hieb-fechten* was found as part of Johann Georg Passcha's 1661 treatise *Kurtze Iedoch Deutliche Beschreibung Handlend von Fechten auff den Stoß und Hieb*. The English translation of both titles is roughly: "A short and clear instruction on cut-fencing."

Henning gives very little information about himself, and he does not purport to be a master. He even includes a poem in his material where he asks his audience to be kind to the fact that his written instructions are brief.

As Henning himself notes, his treatise is brief, but it has several factors making it noteworthy in terms of 17th century Polish saber dueling.

First, it is from the correct century.

Second, it comes from a manual focusing on cutting, rather than the numerous 17th century thrust-orientated Italian treatises.

Third, there is direct mention of the Polish cross-cut.

Before describing the cross-cut, Henning explains counter-cutting that matches the counter-cuts depicted in Heussler's work, including advice on how to perform such techniques safely.

Henning's view on the Polish cross-cut is not a positive one. He places it, almost as an afterthought, in a heading on what to do against a furious and charging opponent. However, his description of cross-cutting, which he calls the Polish, or natural fight, coincides with German dussack material on the cross-cut and Giganti's description of cross-cutting with the rapier.

Kurtze Jedoch Gründliche Unterrichtung vom Hieb-fechten

[excerpts]

by

Erhardus Henning (1658)

English Translation: Reinier van Noort

The twelfth question is, what should I do against someone who likes to counter-cut?

Although here one must take heed, that in cut-fencing the counter-cuts, as the counter-thrusts in thrust-fencing, are the best, if only they are done in the right way and manner, so that absolutely no danger is procured. Which is why, then, many lessons on this have also been reported above. Only when one thinks to counter-cut from desperation, and only intends that one offend his adversary, even though one sets his body in utmost danger, this is wrong and against all justness. And one often tends to call him, who solely has this in mind, by wrongful names. Therefore, when he carries himself such, one can use the following lessons:

I make a half cut[177], if the adversary counter-cuts, I parry, and cut after.

Or I make a half cut, if he cuts along, I let the adversary's cut miss.

Or I myself counter-cut, though such that I hope for no danger with it.

Or I cut half, and on his cut go under him.

Or which is almost the safest to use against someone who counter-cuts. I always engage the blade, and make only slices, such as to the arm, mouth, body, etc. If the adversary then cuts, then I must be ready with defenses such as parrying and letting a cut miss.[178]

The thirteenth question is, what should I do when my adversary comes running in at me with great fury?

Here one must consider, that this is often done out of desperation, and often also out of imprudence. I can therefore encounter him thus.[179]

If he comes running and does not cut, step in the Prime[180] and let him march past, besides give him one on his way, or yield a few steps and cut from me.

---

177   A half-cut is similar to a feint, though Henning describes, though doesn't define, them differently. In Henning's prior descriptions, a half-cut is followed by a half-cut elsewhere.
178   Two of Heussler's plays depict this. A cut to the inside or outside of the arm is met by voiding the cut while cutting the opponent's sword arm.
179   Henning in the prior section scolds someone who strikes with no sense of personal safety and here he explains how best to oppose them.
180   Henning describes four guards; *prime*, *secunde*, *tertie*, and *quarte*, which match the standard rapier guards set down by Agrippa, and used by most rapier masters of the 17th century, such as Capo Ferro and Fabris.

Or go around him, so that he cannot at all come on my body.

Or I hold the point in front of him, thus he runs himself on the sword.[181]

If he comes running and cuts at the same time, the I either let his cut miss, and cut after, or parry the cut and make a lesson, that belongs to the same cut which he has cut.[182]

Or go under him, and give him a dangling.[183]

And here must be noted well that one can also make these same lessons against someone who uses the cross cuts, which fight is indeed held high by some, but is not at all from the art, but can much more be named a natural or Polish fight.

However, one lets everyone remain as he sees fit.

And so much about cut-fencing.

Author's Note Another angle that Henning might have been taking is one on tempo and that those coming furiously, or with the Polish fight, had no regard for it, at least in his view. To men like Henning, and especially Italian masters, such as Giganti, Fabris (with advice on how to bypass the general rules on tempo), and Capo Ferro, tempo was crucial. Perhaps, in Poland, this was not the case, and swift, repeated cross-cuts acted as an offense and defense, or perhaps tempo existed, though it was not called by that name, and Henning didn't recognize it in the Polish fight. As Henning said, "One lets everyone remain as he sees fit."

---

181   This advice is a standard response in Italian rapier treaties and can be found in Giganti's first book.
182   This is further detailed in the prior section on counter-cutting.
183   The translator, Reinier van Noort, notes that the word "dangling" could mean several things. Needless to say, it is an attack of some sort that goes under the opponent's wild attack.

Interpretation

This chapter is an interpretation of the use of the Polish saber of the 17th century in the context of the duel on foot. The prior material has been combined and used to create a coherent system that can be used in isolated training drills or in sparring with a partner.

Lacking a period fencing manual from which to work, knowing how to reconstruct the 17th century Polish system of fencing requires more interpretation than trying to recreate Italian rapier, or German longsword. While there is no definitive period text, the previously detailed sources do provide more than enough material to interpret the system.

Given Poland's ability to adopt and use other customs, the great influx of foreigners, and the loose style of training, it is quite plausible that there was a good deal of personalization in the use of the Polish saber. A nobleman educated in Padua might take up Italian notions such as the concept of tempo and the use of the lunge. Another, who spent time in the Royal army, might pick up different techniques from the many Germans in its ranks. Yet another, who found himself fighting Muscovites, might well devise a system suited toward combating them. Pasek's journals indicate that rapiers, for instance, were used by his fellow Poles. Is it so hard to believe that what they learned about one weapon, they tried to incorporate with another?

Despite the adoption of outside ideas, there was still something unique to the Polish method of fencing. There were enough differences that Father Jezierski, Kitowicz, and Starzewski made note of it. Perhaps, as in the 17th century Polish style of dress and architecture, it was the mixing and matching of the outside world with their own that made it "Polish."

Interpretation is hardly an exact science, and so we must use what sources, anecdotes, and connections are available, and work from there.

Using every source included in this book is not necessary. It is acceptable to pick and choose from what is available, since to date there is nothing more definitive. Furthermore, every source comes with advantages and disadvantages. Starzewski wrote one of the most complete sources, and it is of Polish origin. However, his writings are a 19th century interpretation of the 17th century. Giganti's description of cross-cutting comes from the correct century and lends itself well to the Polish saber and the mysterious cross-cut first mentioned by Father Jezierski. Alas, Giganti's book was written specifically for the use of the rapier and makes no mention of the saber or of Poland. Pasek and Kitowicz give us firsthand accounts, but they give few specifics when it comes to fencing. In the case of Pasek, the memoir was written down years after the actual events took place. All of the sources, be it Pasek, Starzewski, Marcelli, or Meyer, have strengths and weaknesses, and these should be understood before proceeding.

In the end, the goal of an interpretation is to provide as valid a system as possible, while being well aware that newly discovered material, or critical analysis of what is known, may change and alter it.

Concepts of Fencing

To facilitate the interpretation, there are a few core concepts found in numerous systems that are also found in this system. Some of these are based on the ideas of Aristotle, others were set down in later periods by fencing masters.

<u>Definition: Measure</u> = Aristotle used measure as a means of explaining distances between objects. For fencing, the concepts of measure are used to determine, abstractly, how close an opponent is to you.

Measure is relative to the fencers. A tall person with a long sword could be in wide measure while facing a shorter opponent with a shorter sword who might be out of measure, because the taller person would be able to hit while the shorter person would still be out of range.

Measure can be defined in three categories.

Out of Measure

Wide Measure

Close Measure

1- OUT OF MEASURE - Out of range to hit an opponent, even when making a full passing step.

From here, very little matters since neither opponent can attack one another. This changes the moment either fencer enters into wide measure.

2 - WIDE MEASURE - Within range to hit an opponent with an advance or a passing step.

From here, everything matters because each opponent can strike. Every movement, the choice of guard and attack is critical. Additionally, it is possible for one fencer to be in measure, while the other is not.

3 - CLOSE MEASURE - Within range to hit or even to grab an opponent without moving the feet.[184]

From here, not only is the weapon a concern, but the off-hand as well. It is easy to get to grips at this range and a fencer has to worry about being cut or stabbed! At this range both fencers will be in measure.

---

184   Giganti's 17th century rapier treatise used similar concepts of measure. Aaraon Taylor Miedema, *Nicoletto Giganti's The School of the Sword*, (Kingston: Legacy Books Press, 2014), xxiii.

<u>Definition: Tempo</u> = Aristotle measured time through motion. When something moved, a tempo had passed. When something was still, a tempo had passed. When something moved slowly, it was a long tempo, and when something moved quickly, a short one. Two actions were two tempo. Logically, a single tempo action should complete before a two tempo action, and a short tempo should complete before a long tempo.

In fencing, the term is used to understand movement and its relationship to an opportunity to attack or to be attacked. Different masters used tempo differently. Rapier masters of the 17th century tended to suggest a single-time stratagem, where the attack and defense were combined.[185] The small sword of the late 17th to the 19th century often used a double-time system, where an attack was parried and then followed with a counter-attack.[186] In the 18th and 19th century, the development of sport fencing led to quick attacks meant to touch the opponent first.

When using the Polish saber, in a 17th century context, some offensive actions required two tempo to complete, such as a cut powered by a moulinet of the wrist or arm. However, some actions require a single tempo, such as a simple cut, a thrust, or a changing of guard.

The fencer on the right is performing a two tempo action. One to get into the position as depicted, and another will be needed to pass and strike. The fencer on the left can use a hanging parry in response. This will be a one tempo action since all he has to do is raise his arm into the correct position.

---

185   Salvatore Fabris, Capo Ferro and Nicooletto Giganti all depict numerous single-time actions in their rapier manuals.

186   Sir William Hope's manual *The Scots Fencing Master* (1693) and Anthony Gordon's *A Treatise on the Science of Defence for the Sword, Bayonet, and Pike, in Close Action* (1805) both discuss a parry and riposte system.

<u>Definition: Martial Validity</u> = The effect of an attack can be difficult to judge. Things to consider are the power behind an attack and how valid it is.

While single tempo cuts are very fast, they do not always have the power behind them to do damage, and if performed poorly they can leave openings for a counter-attack.[187]

For example, a simple single tempo cut to an opponent's head while he is in the process of making a two tempo moulinet powered by the arm may strike first, but it might not stop the opponent from completing his more powerful (and thus more deadly) attack.[188] However, if a simple single tempo cut is directed at an opponent's head while he is in the process of advancing, this is a much better situation. Because the fencer is not at risk, and can safely guard himself after he strikes, the attack can be considered martially valid.

To fence well, measure, tempo and martial validity need to be combined. Ideally, the objective is to hit and not be hit until the opponent is no longer a threat.

The fencer on the right is preparing a powerful, arm-powered moulinet. The fencer on the left could attempt a quick simple cut to his head, but would likely be struck by the much more powerful incoming attack as he did so. The fencers have to try to hit well, and hit and not be hit. This is a continual balancing act of movement, guards, attacks, parries and counter-attacks!

---

187   The issue of martially valid cuts remained an issue well into the modern era. Giueseppe Radaelli re-introduced powerful cuts into the Italian military because, as General Angelini noted in 1888, the prior system which used only wrist moulinets hampered the effectiveness of the saber. Christopher Holzman, *The Art of the Dueling Sabre*, (New York: SKA Swordplay Books, 2011), xxvi.

188   Settimo Del Frate, whose textbook was based on Radaelli, warned that such attacks done too soon or too late left the fencer in danger of being struck. Ibid, 16.

Some questions to consider are:

Measure

1- Am I in range to be hit by my opponent?

2- Am I in range to hit my opponent?

3- Am I in range to use my off-hand to grab my opponent?

Tempo

1- If I move or change position, will I be struck?

2- If I do nothing, will I be struck?

3- If my opponent moves or changes position, can I strike?

4- If my opponent does nothing, can I strike?

5- Can I respond with a defense if my opponent attacks?

6- Can my opponent respond with a defense if I attack?

Martial Validity

1- If I strike, will I be struck back?

2- Will my strike have enough power behind it to do damage? Example: A light hit to the body is different than a light strike to the fingers.

3- Is my opponent's strike something that has enough power behind it to do damage? Example: A light gesture toward the head is likely a feint.

<u>Definition</u>: <u>The Line</u> = Between two opponents is an imaginary line that runs between their feet, from one fencer to the other. It is the quickest way for the opponents to close upon each other, which also makes it a dangerous line since they can both strike one another swiftly along this line. A common tactic is to attack or defend in such a way as to move off the line, either when attacking or defending.[189]

THE LINE

DEFINITION: INSIDE AND OUTSIDE = For the right-handed fencer, everything from left of the sword is the inside and everything to the right is the outside.

For example, if an opponent is wearing a wristwatch, an attack at the opponent's right wrist where the face of the watch would show, is an attack to the outside of the wrist. An attack at the opponent's right wrist where the strap of the watch would buckle is an attack to the inside of the wrist.

Inside and outside is respective of the fencer and the opponent. A fencer can perform an inside wrist moulinet directed at the outside of the opponent. He could also perform the same attack to the inside of the opponent.

OUTSIDE   INSIDE

Stances and Movement

TOES FORWARD = This stance can be seen in Almonte's painting depicting Polish youths engaged in *palcaty*. It is a broader stance, with the toes of both feet pointed toward the opponent.

TOES OPPOSITE = This stance, depicted in dussack manuals, has the rear foot pointed away from the opponent.[190] The stance is broad, to allow the use of the off-hand as well as facilitate off-line movement. The weight can be even, or on the lead or rear foot.

---

190   Seen in Mair, Meyer and Sutor.

STARZEWSKI INITIAL = This variation of the "toes opposite" stance has the heels in line and the weight resting on the rear foot, with the body sinking slightly lower by bending at the knees.

In this stance, the left foot has all the strength – and it is placed just so: when I have my right foot facing forward and in front of me – the left is placed in a half turn behind me, so that the left heel is away from the right heel at the distance of about eight inches.

In such a stance, the hand which holds the weapon is dropped down away from my right leg, and I pierce my opponent with a cold gaze, eying him up and down. Thus, I await the attack, or initiate it myself. Michał Starzewski

STARZEWSKI FACING = This stance is the same as the "Starzewski initial," but the knees bend further, lowering the body and reducing the profile even more.

The Facing stance in the Polish school should be as follows: do not change your initial stance at all, but go softer and lower on the legs, suck in your stomach, extend your arm and puff up your chest behind it, and raise the tempered [as in: tempered steel] tip of your kord so that it points at your opponent's right eye, and always keep it pointed at his eyes! And look at him from beneath the crossguard! And so: your knuckleguard will always protect your temple – the straight elbow will save you from a cut, and the moulinet done in time will protect your chest. - Michał Starzewski

LEANING

By bending at the waist it is possible to lean toward an opponent to make a strike, or away from an opponent to avoid their attack. Stances with the toes pointing opposite directions allow for greater leaning than the toes forward stance because the knees can assist by bending and retaining balance.

From Meyer's 1560 manual: a demonstration of leaning forward and backwards.[191]

191   Copy of Meyer dussack plates by Ksenia Kozhevnikova.

FORWARD MOVEMENT

ADVANCE = The lead foot extends and the rear foot follows. This should be done as smoothly as possible to prevent bobbing of the head. A deceptive way to advance is to move the rear foot closer to the lead foot and then to advance the lead foot. This gains a surprising amount of ground.

PASS = A pass is a slower way to move forward, but it covers more ground by having the rear foot step forward to become the new lead foot. The pass also allows off-line movement by stepping at an angle.

Backward Movement

Retreat = The rear foot steps back and the lead foot follows. This can be done quite effectively by pushing off from the lead foot. An alternative method is to move the lead foot first, bringing it closer to the rear foot, and then pushing off from the newly-placed front foot to move the rear foot further back.

Pass-Back = A pass-back is an effective way to increase measure with an opponent or to slip the front leg if it is attacked. The lead foot steps behind and becomes the new rear foot.

LATERAL MOVEMENT

RIGHT = The lead foot moves a little forward and to the right. The rear foot follows.

LEFT = The rear foot moves a little forward and to the left. The lead foot follows. Alternatively (assuming a right foot forward stance), the lead foot can move left, but if the movement is too deep then the legs will become crossed and balance may be affected negatively.

PASS = The pass can be lateral by taking the rear foot and stepping with it diagonally away from the opponent.

Holding the Sword

The saber is to be held in a "locked key" fashion, by inserting the index finger in that hollow which is found in its cross,[192] so that the grip is fast and secure, able to resist violent action, and one doesn't lose the grip on it, which could easily happen, if one held it in another way, or tried to play with it like he was using a rapier. Antoinio Marcelli

This finger aids the thumb in all its workings; it also leads all the cuts, and as such is called the leading finger; and because quite often it is put into the ring or loop, we can also call it the ring finger. Michał Starzewski

Marcelli refers to the most secure grip of the saber as the Locked-Key grip, and this correlates with Starzewski's advice. In this grip, the hand makes a solid fist around the hilt, while the thumb is placed through a thumb-ring (if present), or pressed tightly against the knuckles of the index finger.[193] Both Starzewski and Marcelli make reference to a loop, possibly a leather loop, for the index finger. When moving the sword, the thumb and index finger help to direct it. When actually making a cut, the middle, ring, and pinky fingers can tighten upon the hilt to deliver more strength into the attack.

---

192   Maybe it's a finger ring in this case, this would suggest an Italian *Storta* is the weapon Marcelli writes about. -Translator's note-

193   Starzewski refers to the index finger as the "ring finger."

Heussler depicts the occasional use of a much looser grip, where the thumb and index finger are pinching the hilt and the last three fingers are loose. This can gain range in an attack, but should be used sparingly because it is not a secure way to grip the sword and is susceptible to beats.

The left hand, or off-hand as it is also called, can be placed on the hip, open along the back, tucked in a belt by the thumb near the stomach, or limp and near the chest. The left hand can be used to come to grips with an opponent, but otherwise should stay out of the fight so as not to be struck incidentally.[194]

194   Rapier masters such as Fabris described the use of the left hand. However, with a saber, any attempt to grab a moving blade would likely result in missing fingers. Grabs should be to the opponent's arm or wrist.

Guards

Guards are positions to hold the sword. They are places from which to attack and defend. Normally, the right foot is leading to maximize range and to present the side of the body that is most defended. However, on occasion, the left foot might lead, such as when passing back. Stance is combined with the guards, allowing for a multitude of dynamic variations. The following guards are derived from source material, but given different names to prevent a mix of terminology.

HIGH EXTENDED[195] = The sword's point is directed at the opponent's face or upper body.

The knuckles are turned to the sky, while the arm is slightly bent so that the shoulder can bear some of the weight. The sword is held high enough to protect the head. This guard can strain the arm, but presents a threat to the opponent at the maximum measure.

Sutor and Meyer's Bogen or Bow for dussack, and Meyer's Right Ox for rapier.[196]

---

195   Similar to the *Bogen* guard for dussack and the *Ox* for rapier found in Meyer. The "high extended" guard is also used as an engaging guard in saber treatises such as Angelo's *Infantry Sword Exercise* of 1817, and is similar to Starzewski's "Facing Stance." Sutor image provided by Keith P. Myers, copy of Meyer dussack plates by Ksenia Kozhevnikova.

196   Images provided by Kevin Maurer and Keith P. Myers.

The "high extended" guard existed in later periods, such as this depiction from an 1843 Russian saber manual in which the guard was shown as the first position to attain upon drawing the weapon from its sheathe.[197]

197   *An Outline of the Rules of Fencing, With Sketches, In Five Parts*. By the Assistant to the Principal Fencing-master of the Separate Corps of Guards, St. Petersburg, Sokolov, 1843, http://www.reenactor.ru/ARH/Drill/Pravila_Fext_1843.pdf, accessed 3-19-2014

HIGH RETRACTED[198] = From the "high extended" guard, the elbow is bent, withdrawing the point away from the opponent. The retracted guard is less fatiguing than the extended and can be used deceptively.

Meyer depicts the Stier or steer guard where the sword is high and retracted and the left hand is raised, gripping the dussack. In our interpretation, the left hand is kept away from the blade and either on the hip, behind the back, or near the chest or belt.[199]

HIGH OVER THE SHOULDER[200] = The sword arm is drawn back and high so the false edge of the

---

198   Similar to the *Stier* guard found in Meyer and Sutor, but with the left hand not gripping the wrist.

199   Copy of Meyer dussack plates by Ksenia Kozhevnikova.

200   Known in Meyer and Sutor as a *Zornhut* or Wrath Guard.

blade rests upon the right shoulder. Alternatively, the false edge could rest on the left shoulder, but this exposes the right arm to attack.

Woodcut by Lucas Mayer, 1595, depicting Polish and Habsburg forces. Using a high and over the shoulder guard, men in Polish attire herd prisoners. Interestingly enough, the Poles are depicted as left-handed and the Habsburg forces as right.[201]

---

201   Dariusz Caballeros, http://dariocaballeros.blogspot.com/2011/01/lucas-mayer-woodcuts-1595-96-war-fare-in.html accessed, 3-9-2014.

MIDDLE GUARD[202] = The sword is held in front of the body with the tip pointed to the sky. The arm is bent and the elbow does not stick out. From here all the parries are achieved easily and it is a good guard in which to wait and to which to return.

Meyer describes this as a straight parry. The individual is dressed in Polish attire.[203]

---

202   Meyer and Sutor both describe the *schnitt* or straight parry as a parry or guard from which the long edge is facing the opponent and the arm is extended.

203   Copy of Meyer dussack plates by Ksenia Kozhevnikova.

The Middle Guard existed in later periods, such as this depiction from a 1799 British saber manual, written by Henry Angelo and sketched by Thomas Rowlandson in which the guard was known as the Medium Guard.[204]

---

204   Thomas Rowlandson, 1799. *Hungarian and Highland Broadsword*. HEW 9.13.22, Harry Elkins Widener Collection, Harvard University, courtesy Michael Chidester.

LOW GUARD TRUE[205] = The sword is held low, with the hilt near the right knee and the point of the blade pointed at the ground. This guard invites an attack to the head, which can be thwarted by transitioning into a hanging guard.

The stance is back weighted in this image, but it is perfectly plausible for the weight to be forward or evenly distributed depending on the situation.[206]

---

205   This guard can be found in Mair's description of dussack.
206   Copy of Mair dussack plate by Mariana López-Rodríguez.

LOW GUARD FALSE[207] = By cutting from the high over the shoulder guard toward the ground, this guard can be achieved. The false edge of the blade is prepared for a deflection against incoming attacks.

This guard can be achieved by starting in the high over the shoulder guard and cutting all the way through, down to the ground. The false edge is facing the opponent.

---

207   Meyer describes this guard as *Wechsel* or "Changer."

HIGH EXTENDED

High Retracted

HIGH OVER THE SHOULDER

MIDDLE GUARD

LOW GUARD TRUE

LOW GUARD FALSE

Parries

Parries are meant to stop incoming attacks. Once a parry is made, either a counter-attack should be launched, or a guard should be adopted. Parries are performed with the edge of the saber, and have more strength near the guard, less near the tip.[208] An easy way to remember the parries is to consider them as components to a house. They consist of hanging, straight and low parries.

ROOF = The house needs to shield itself from the rain and to direct it away. There are two hanging parries that can be adopted: one with the point to the right (outside), the other with the point to the left (inside). These hanging parries are angled so that incoming attacks slide off them. The more strength and forward momentum an attack has, the more easily it is deflected, and it provides the energy for a counter-attack.

WALLS = The house needs to be roomy and have sturdy walls. The curve of a saber can be used to turn the blade around a parry and bring the point to a threatening place. To prevent an opponent from performing this trick, straight parries to the left and right are made with an extended arm.

FLOOR = The floors of the house need to match the walls. The true edge is used to block low attacks. As with the straight parries, these low parries need to have the arm extended so an opponent cannot use the curve of their saber to strike around the guard.

208   Marcelli states that the entire saber is considered strong, from the *forte* to the *debole*. This is because his manual deals with the rapier opposed to the saber, not two sabers in opposition.

ELEMENTS OF THE ROOF: HANGING PARRIES (OUTSIDE AND INSIDE)

ELEMENTS OF THE WALLS: STRAIGHT PARRIES (OUTSIDE AND INSIDE)

Elements of the Floor: Low Parries (Outside and Inside)

Attacks

Attacks come in two varieties: the cut and the thrust. The saber is designed to be a cutting weapon, and while it can thrust, that is not its primary purpose. To attack safely, the prior lessons of measure, tempo, martial validity and the line need to be understood.

ORDER = To safely attack, the saber must lead, and the body and foot should follow.

To perform a simple cut, the arm extends, and with that the saber moves forward. The body then leans toward the opponent. Finally, the right foot advances. Ideally, the cut hits the opponent at the same time as the right foot finishes moving. In this way, the foot and body power the saber, but the saber is always leading so that it provides protection should something go wrong.

When recovering from an attack, the order is reversed. The foot moves, then the body, followed by the saber. In this way, the saber remains as a defense, while the foot and body retract.

Tightening the Bottom Fingers = By tightening the bottom three fingers just before a cut lands, more power can be provided. In other situations, the bottom three fingers are loose, so moulinets can be easily performed and different grips of the saber adopted.

SIMPLE CUT = The simple cut is the fastest (single tempo), but also the weakest. Because it is fast, it has the smallest of tempos. To perform a simple cut, the arm extends and with it the saber. The body then leans toward the opponent. The right foot advances. Ideally, the cut hits the opponent at the same time the right foot finishes moving. It is also possible to make a passing step; this should be done off the line, and the order remains the same.

WRIST MOULINET = The wrist-powered moulinet is moderately fast (short two tempo) and more powerful. Because it takes longer to execute, there is more risk involved in using it; however it strikes with more force. To perform a wrist moulinet, the saber moves in a circle. The arm should be stationary while the circle is made, relying on the wrist to generate the motion. The bottom three fingers can be loose to aid in manipulating the blade. As the saber comes back around, it will have more momentum and from there is treated like a simple cut. The saber is already moving, the body then leans and the foot follows, with the cut and foot ideally landing at the same time. The wrist moulinet can use the true edge, but also the false edge, in which case the tip acts like a sharp beak to pierce the opponent's wrist or hand. It is also possible to make a passing step when performing this attack; this should be done off the line, while the order remains the same.

ARM MOULINET = The arm-powered moulinet is the slowest (long two tempo) but most powerful of attacks. It takes the longest to execute, and there is more risk of counter-attack during it, but it strikes with the most power. As the arm rises over the head, there is a moment of vulnerability and the fencer should be keenly aware of this. To perform an arm moulinet the saber is raised over the head, as if performing a hanging parry to the left. The saber then makes a circle behind the head. As the saber comes around with great speed and power, it becomes a simple cut. Once more, the saber leads the attack, followed by a lean of the body and finally the foot. It is very acceptable to pass while conducting this attack.

THRUST = A thrust is performed by extending the blade so the point is directed at the opponent. It is possible to do this from the Middle Guard, so that the true edge is facing the ground, or from one of the high guards so that the true edge is facing the sky. It is also possible to turn any of the cuts into a thrust at the moment of contact with an opponent's blade, by rotating the wrist so that the point strikes. The order is the same as cuts, with the sword moving first, then the body, and the foot ideally landing as the thrust makes contact.

FEINT[209] = Giganti's 1606 rapier treatise describes a feint in the most simple of terms. Feinting means motioning to do one thing and doing another.[210] The feint needs to be performed in such a manner that if the opponent does not respond they can still be hit.

INTENTION = When an attack is meant to hit, it is a first intention, because the attacker *intended* to connect. When an attack is a feint, then strikes elsewhere it is a second intention, because the second attack was *intended* to hit. It is possible to have subsequent intentions.[211]

209   The best way to perform a feint was contested in the early 17th century. Capo Ferro indicated feinting is not good (though he depicts it often). Giganti is terse in his writing and has no strong opinion, while Fabris is verbose and details good and bad ways to feint. In the late 19th century Frate and Hutton described feints in similar terms in that they had to be believable or they would expose the fencer to risk.

210   Tom Leoni, *Venetian Rapier,* (Wheaton: Freelance Academy Press, 2010), 13.

211   This is an older, 19th century, interpretation of intention. Modern sport fencing uses the second intention to elicit a specific parry. Christopher Holzman, *The Art of the Dueling Sabre*, (New York: SKA Swordplay Books, 2011), 13.

Simple Cut

Wrist Moulinet (A cut from the outside)

Wrist Moulinet (A cut from the inside)

Wrist Moulinet (Using the false edge)

WRIST MOULINET (DETAIL)

Arm Moulinet

THRUST (STRAIGHT)

THRUST (INSIDE OF THE OPPONENT'S SABER)

THRUST (OUTSIDE OF THE OPPONENT'S SABER)

Thrust (Over the opponent's saber)

Targets

BODY = Starzewski's cutting diagram for deep cuts, or the core, breaks down the possible targets for attack as top, middle, and bottom.[212]

Above

A descending right to left cut aimed at the opponent's left shoulder and arm and delivered so as to cut into the body.

A cut to the brow.[213]

A descending left to right cut aimed at the opponent's right shoulder and arm and delivered so as to cut into the body.

Middle

A descending right to left cut into the opponent's left cheek.

A horizontal right to left cut into the opponent's left armpit.

An ascending right to left cut into the opponent's left hip.

A descending left to right cut into the opponent's right cheek.[214]

A horizontal left to right cut into where the neck and head join.

An ascending left to right cut into the opponent's right hip.

Bottom

An ascending cut into the opponent's right side or groin.

An ascending cut from below.[215]

An ascending cut into the opponent's left side.

---

212   The cutting diagram is similar to that of Meyer's dussack.
213   Daria Izdebska translated this cut as *wbrew*, meaning brow or forehead. Starzewski does not describe it in the text but shows it in his cutting diagram.
214   Starzewski states the "left eye," but this may mean cutting through the face to reach it. The cut to the other side is aimed at the left cheek.
215   Daria Izdebska translates this cut as *wpion*, which means "in-vertical" and is a cut from directly below.

Red lines indicate descending attacks. *Blue lines* indicate horizontal attacks. *Green lines* indicate ascending attacks. *The lines are directed through the targets laid out by Starzewski.*

Hand = Starzewski depicts a diagram for strikes to the hand that are divided into top, middle and bottom.[216]

Top

A descending cut from right to left into the top of the opponent's hand.

A descending cut from above into the top of the opponent's hand, directed at the top of the wrist.

A descending cut from left to right into the top of the opponent's hand, directed at the index finger.

Middle

A horizontal cut from right to left into the palm of the opponent.

A horizontal cut from left to right into the fingers holding the grip of the saber.

Bottom

An ascending cut from right to left into the bottom of the opponent's hand, directed at the pinky.

An ascending cut from below into the bottom of the opponent's hand, directed at where the wrist and pommel meet.

An ascending cut from left to right into the bottom of the opponent's hand.

---

216   Starzewski's 19th century diagram and explanation for detailed strikes to the hand has no period-equivalent. Dussack, rapier and side-sword cutting diagrams on the head and body. That said, in the context of a duel, a strike to the hand was more common, as seen in Zabłocki's research of first-hand accounts and mentioned with some wistful lament by Kitowicz.

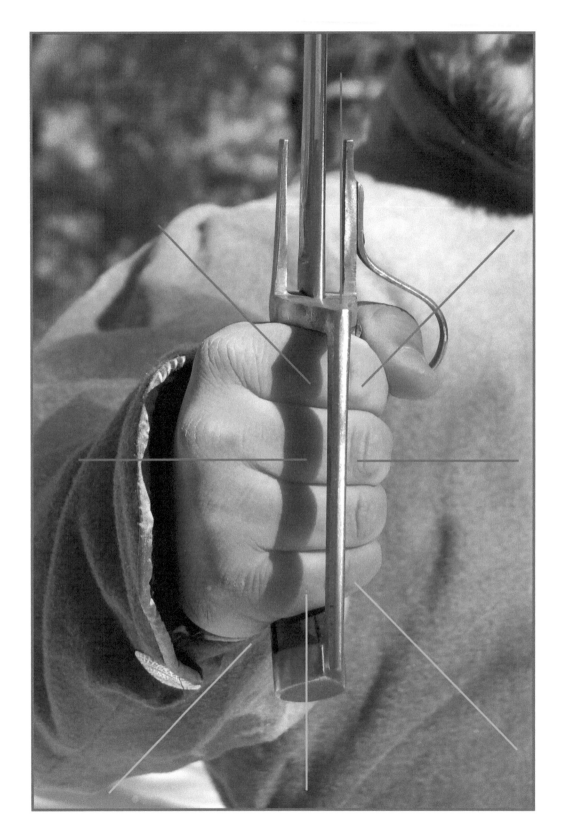

Red lines indicate descending attacks. *Blue lines* indicate horizontal attacks. *Green lines* indicate ascending attacks. The lines are directed through the targets laid out by Starzewski.

Techniques

Response to an Unskilled, Powerful Attack.

The giants, who were very heavy men and not very good at saber, did not know a single fencing sequence, but always came at the guardsmen from above, as if using flails. In response the guardsmen came in underneath, quickly and smoothly, marked the giants on the face, then retreated. - Jędrzej Kitowicz

Treatises often depict how to oppose an untrained opponent. Fiore de Liberi's treatise on medieval combat refers to such an attack as the "Villain's Blow". Capo Ferro refers to such an opponent as bestial, while Fabris describes him as hot blooded. Henning and Giganti both discuss how to oppose a fencer with no thought toward their own safety, who keeps advancing with powerful attacks. Kitowicz's anecdote about the Polish response to such an opponent is to cut under their slow, telegraphed attack, aiming at their face, and then to retreat.

Timing is important. As Henning's brief instructions on cut-fencing noted, counter-cutting has to be done with skill to avoid injury. However, an unskilled opponent's attack will be exaggerated. During the tempo in which the opponent raises their arm, they can be struck. As their arm descends with the powerful cut, they can be avoided with a retreat.

RESPONSE TO AN UNSKILLED, POWERFUL ATTACK

Red awaits in the "Low Guard True" position to receive a powerful attack from his larger, but unskilled, opponent, white. As white attacks, red moves laterally to the right, voiding the attack. Simultaneously, red performs a cut at white's face. For safety, red then passes back and prepares for the next action.

HANGING PARRIES

The hanging parry is angled so blows slide off it like rain to the inside or outside. When an opponent strikes with power, the hanging parry can be used to deflect the attack to the right or left depending on which hanging parry is used.

When an opponent has forward momentum as well as power in their attack, the hanging parry can be used in conjunction with a step. In this way the blow is deflected and the opponent is opened up for a counter-attack.

MIDDLE GUARD USING THE INSIDE HANGING PARRY

White attacks red, trying to cut his right cheek. Red is waiting in the "Middle Guard" and responds with an inside hanging parry. The force of white's cut will cause his blade to slide off the roof that red has created with his parry. Red counters with a cut to white's neck.

MIDDLE GUARD USING THE OUTSIDE HANGING PARRY

White attacks, directing a cut at red's left cheek. Red uses the outside hanging parry to intercept the attack and allow it to slide off his roof. At the same time, red passes forward at an angle. Red now has an opportunity to counter-attack, and uses his left hand to secure white's wrist, while delivering a cut of his own.

LOW GUARD TRUE USING THE INSIDE HANGING PARRY

White strikes at red's head, an open target, since red waits in the "Low Guard True." Red performs an inside hanging parry. The force of white's strike causes it to slide off the roof that has been created. Red counter-attacks with a cut directed at white's neck.

Low Guard True using the outside hanging parry

White strikes at red's head, an open target, since red waits in the "Low Guard True." Red uses the outside hanging parry to intercept the attack and allow it to slide off his roof. At the same time, red passes forward at an angle. Red now has an opportunity to counter-attack, and uses his left hand to secure white's wrist, while delivering a cut of his own.

Detail of grip

RESPONSE TO A PARRY

Single-time actions, which are so important with the rapier, are very dangerous with the saber, because it is a cutting weapon and cannot hit the opponent with the edge and set aside his blade at the same time: offence doesn't defend at the same time, so you cannot offend in single time. - Antonio Marcelli

Marcelli suggests that the saber should be used in double- rather than single-time. To fence in double-time is to parry an attack and respond with a counter-attack, or to initiate an attack and then to strike elsewhere after the attack is parried. It is a technique common to saber and cut-fencing. When an opponent attacks, it takes a tempo for them to recover, and this provides an opening for a counter-attack. Conversely, if an opponent is attacked and parries, an opportunity arises to strike them before they can act.

AN ATTACK IS USED TO DRAW OUT A PARRY

White and red both are using the "Middle Guard." Red attacks white's left side to draw out a parry. As soon as this is accomplished, he passes forward and cuts at white's unprotected right side.

Using the Curve

At the onset, use the Weckerhau (waking strike) like this: strike into him with a powerful Oberhau. He parries the strike, so at the same time that his parry touches, wind the strike into a thrust by pushing your Dusack around and inward into his face. - Jacob Sutor

The curve of the saber can be used to defeat an opponent's hanging parry or an improper parry. After the parry makes contact with the saber's true edge, the saber can be turned so its false edge comes into contact with the opponent's saber. The curve of the saber allows it now to thrust around the poorly formed parry, or over the hanging parry. A poorly formed parry is one that is made too close to the body.

THRUSTING OVER A HANGING PARRY

White forms a hanging parry either due to a feint from red, or perhaps using it as a guard. Red responds by thrusting so that the false edge of his blade comes into contact with white's saber. The curve of red's saber allows him to plunge his thrust over white's parry and into white's chest.

THRUSTING AROUND A PARRY TO THE OUTSIDE

Red attacks white's outside shoulder. White's parry is not wide enough, so red turns his wrist and his thrust goes around white's blade and into white's chest. The same tactic could be accomplished if red attacked white from the inside and white's inside parry was not properly formed.

A PROPERLY FORMED INSIDE PARRY

White attempts a cut at red's inside. Red parries, keeping his arm far enough out and turning his body to ensure that white cannot turn his wrist and try to thrust around the parry.

A PROPERLY FORMED OUTSIDE PARRY

White attempts a cut at red's outside. Red parries, keeping his arm far enough out and turning his body to ensure that white cannot turn his wrist and try to thrust around the parry.

CROSS CUTTING

The Cross Cuts are essentially two Wrath Cuts from both sides; they are executed through the two downward angling lines that run through the opponent diagonally from both sides, and cross over one another. - Joachim Meyer

The mandritto and roverscio therefore attack in the form of a cross. With this method you both attack and defend since your sword must inevitably find your enemies' weapon. Note that these mandrittti and roversci should be delivered long, hard, quickly, and without ever stopping. - Nicoletto Giganti

...and the Pole uses cross cuts. - Salezy Jezierski

The cross cut is essential to Polish saber-fencing. Unfortunately, there is no clear definition of what cross cutting is in the Polish sources of the 17th century. Salezy Jezierski marks it as unique to the Poles. German masters of the 16th century describe cross cutting as a technique used with the dussack, cutting from one direction and then another. Giganti shows it as a method to deflect an incoming cut from right-to-left and countering with a cut from left-to-right. Henning calls it the Polish, or natural, fight and is derisive, stating that it is separate from the art of cut-fencing altogether. Our interpretation is that cross cutting is two cuts in the form of an X. While simplistic at first glance, there are numerous variations of cross-cutting that can make it an art of its own.

CROSS CUT AS A BEAT

The mandritto should be delivered so it almost wounds your enemy's neck, and finishes ready to attack again from the left. In this manner the mandritto has two effects, it offends and protects at the same time. Having delivered the mandritto you should bring your body back and foot back, put the sword under your left arm ready for the roverscio, then quickly execute this roverscio as follows. It should begin by attacking your opponent's neck, and end once more on your right side. The mandritto and roverscio therefore attack in the form of a cross. - Nicoletto Giganti

In this technique, a strong, right-to-left cut is directed at the opponent's sword and neck while extending the lead foot. Afterwards, the lead foot and body retract, and a left-to-right cut is directed at the opponent's neck. This forms the cross, which both offends and defends, and can be performed in repetition.

CROSS CUT AS A BEAT (PART 1)

White and red stand in the "High Over the Shoulder Guard." White attacks, and in response, red extends his lead foot and performs a powerful right-to-left cut meant to beat aside his opponent's sword. Red finishes the cut by entering the "High Over the Shoulder Guard" on the other side, while withdrawing his lead foot.

CROSS CUT AS A BEAT (PART 2)

After performing a right-to-left cut, moving from one "High Over the Shoulder Guard" to the other, red performs a left-to-right cut returning to his original guard. The technique can be repeated, with the lead foot extending and retracting as red cuts from right-to-left then left-to-right.

CROSS CUT AS A FEINT

You can use feints in saber play, although it's not so easy, by pretending to cut a target and cutting another instead. - Antonio Marcelli

A cut is delivered from the right, and as soon as the opponent parries, a second cut is made from the left. This is a second intention attack.

Another variation.

The attacker feints a mandritto tondo to the hip, the defender tries to parry it, not being able to slip it, opposing the forte of the sword, however, since the attacker does not commit to that cut, the defender gets hit, in the same time, in the head by a riverso. - Antonio Marcelli

A cut is delivered from right-to-left toward the opponent's hip. When they attempt to parry, the attacker pulls up into a left-to-right cut directed at the opponent's head.

CROSS CUT AS A FEINT (PART 1)

White and red stand in the "Middle Guard." Red performs an arm moulinet threatening to cut from right-to-left. This is done to draw out a hanging parry from white.

CROSS CUT AS A FEINT (PART 2)

After threatening a right-to-left cut with an arm moulinet, red has drawn out a hanging parry from white. When white raises his arm to parry, red makes a passing step and cuts from left-to-right, targeting white's exposed arm. If white had not parried at all, then red could have completed his original arm moulinet.

CROSS CUT AS A FEINT (ANOTHER VARIATION)

White and red stand in the "Middle Guard." Red attacks white's left side. When white attempts to parry, red swiftly cuts toward white's right cheek. As before, if white does not parry, then the attack continues and hits.

Voiding the Leg

When one strikes for your leg, withdraw the foot that is forward or return it behind, and throw a downward blow to his head... - Fiore de'i Liberi, 15th century.

...to strike beneath the waist, or at the legs, is a great disadvantage, because the course of the blow to the legs is too far, & thereby the head, face & body is discovered. - George Silver, 16th century.

While the enemy is descending to wound you, then take your forward leg away backwards. He being unable to ward, wounds himself... - Nicoletto Giganti, 17th century.

... your adversary changes to cut on the outside of your leg;--slip back the right foot to the left heel--your point parallel with the left shoulder, seeing your adversary through the angle, beneath your sword: ---bring your left hand to support the sword-arm, in which attitude you are ready to riposte upon him, and are perfectly secure from his attack. - George Sinclair, 18th century.

...in all cuts at the leg, when at the proper distance, the shifting of your own leg, and delivering a cut at the same moment, becomes the most effective and advantageous defense. - Infantry Sword Exercise, 19th century.

The response to an attack directed at the leg is well-documented throughout the centuries. As the opponent extends themselves to reach the lead leg, you shift the leg back out of measure, or pass back to safety. At the same time, a strike is delivered at the opponent whose head and arm become exposed.

VOIDING THE LEG

White and red stand in the "Middle Guard." White attempts a cut directed at red's leading leg. Red draws his leg back while at the same time bending at the waist and cutting white's head.

Voiding the Body

...to lean forward (towards the brow), you should bend your front knee – and when you retreat, you should bend your back knee. Practice this moving back and forth continually, so that it can become graceful and agile, natural, and – above all – appropriate to your own strengths. - Michał Starzewski

...if your enemy delivers a cut to your head, in the same tempo you should pull your body back... let his cut pass harmlessly.... the harder your enemy cuts, the more he exposes himself, and the harder it is for him to recover. - Nicoletto Giganti

When an opponent cuts at the head or body, the other fighter can void it by leaning back. While the opponent attempts to recover, a counter-attack can take place in the form of a cut or thrust.

> **"Thus, the entire fencing art should rely on the nimble and agile movements of our body."**
> **- Michał Starzewski**

VOIDING THE BODY

White and red stand in the "Middle Guard." White cuts at red's body. In response, red leans back, then swiftly leans forward and cuts at white as white's blade misses its target.

VOIDING AN INSIDE CUT

If one cuts in at you, inside (of your blade) and he will also cut inside to your head, thus pay careful attention to those of his incoming cuts, that you step back with your left foot, and best him in the Measure, and also sink well backwards with your upper body, and cut simultaneous with him inside to his right arm... - Sebastian Heussler

This technique is best performed by moving the rear foot back and a little to the right, so that the heels are in line and the attack is voided. At the same time, a cut is directed at the inside of the opponent's arm.

168

VOIDING AN INSIDE CUT

Red and white stand in the "Middle Guard." White cuts at red's inside. Red responds by simultaneously swinging his rear foot to the right, sinking back and cutting at white's exposed arm.

VOIDING AN OUTSIDE CUT

If one cuts in at you but outside your blade, to your head also, thus pay careful attention that you step well back with your left foot, from his cuts, and cut simultaneously with him outside to his right arm...
- Sebastian Heussler

This technique is performed by moving the rear foot back and a little to the left, so the attack is voided. At the same time a cut is directed at the outside of the opponent's arm.

VOIDING AN OUTSIDE CUT

Red and white stand in the "Middle Guard." White cuts at red's outside. Red responds by simultaneously swinging his rear foot to the left, sinking back and cutting at white's exposed arm.

Voiding while Performing a Moulinet with the False Edge

As the opponent attacks, pass forward at an angle to void the attack. At the same time a reverse moulinet using the false edge rotates the sword away from the opponent's blade. This voids blade contact. Complete the moulinet by striking the opponent's wrist or hand with the false edge near the tip of the saber.

Voiding while performing a moulinet with the false edge

Red and white stand in the "Middle Guard." As white attacks, red makes a passing step to the side while performing a wrist moulinet, using the false edge of his saber to hit white's hand.

Voiding with a Pass

So you use a low cut, that is from the right and below, into the stomach. - Michał Starzewski

Jump backward and sideways, and cut at him with the following cuts: – into his groin or belly from the right below... - Michał Starzewski

This is a rendition of what Starzewski labeled as the *Hellish Polish Fourth*. As the opponent attacks, perform a pass at an angle to void the attack (or jump to the side and back) while responding with a cut aimed at the opponent's stomach, that comes up beneath the opponent's sword.

THE POLISH HELLISH 4TH

Red and white stand in the "Middle Guard." Red passes forward at an angle and delivers a cut from right-to-left under white's saber. By passing well off the line, red voids white's attack.

Voiding the Hand

From the Middle Guard, the arm is extended and the outside of it is exposed, to invite an attack. As the opponent cuts, the arm is retracted to void the strike, while the sword performs a moulinet to void the opponent's sword. Striking the opponent's exposed hand completes the moulinet. The technique works with the same principles as voiding the body. The stronger the opponent cuts, the longer it will take them to recover when they miss their target.

Another variation is if the opponent attempts to beat aside the sword. Again, the hand retracts, and as the opponent's sword misses its intended target, respond with an inside wrist moulinet aimed at the opponent's exposed arm.

Voiding the hand (Part 1)

White and red stand in the "Middle Guard." White attempts to beat aside red's saber, or he could try to strike red's hand. In either case, red retracts his hand so that white misses his target.

Voiding the hand (Part 2)

White has attempted to strike at red's saber or hand. Red has voided this. Before white can recover, red performs an inside wrist moulinet and strikes at white's exposed arm.

SIMPLE BEAT

It happens that your opponent doesn't dare coming in distance to strike, but throws strikes from out of distance to keep you at bay. In such a case, you can parry, stepping in the same time, in order to get closer to the opponent and hit him with a cutting riposte. - Antonio Marcelli

Λ beat is when a cut is directed at the opponent's sword to displace it. Marcelli describes it as a parry while stepping against a rapier. The same can be used against a saber. The beat needs sufficient force to knock the opponent's blade aside, and is followed up with a cut.

SIMPLE BEAT

Red and white stand in the "Middle Guard." Red strikes at white's sword to beat it aside. Red follows up with a passing step and a cut at white's head.

LOW GUARD DEFLECTIONS

Standing in the "Low Guard False," wait for the opponent to cut. Then bring the saber up to the "High Over the Shoulder Guard," using the false edge to deflect the attack aside. Follow up with a passing step and an arm moulinet with a cut directed at the opponent.

Another variation.

> *...pay attention to whether he will strike at your head from his right towards your left. If so, wind with a hanging Dussack the long edge upwards against his strike and at the same time as the parry step with your left foot behind your right away from his strike and let his blow go off of your long edge downward near to your left. Then step with the right foot further to his left and strike forward through his face.* - Jacob Sutor

From the "Low Guard False," wait for the opponent to cut and bring the saber up to the "High Over the Shoulder Guard," using the true edge to deflect the attack aside while passing back. Follow up with a pass forward and a strike.

Another variation.

> *Shove this away crosswise with your short edge. Then immediately set upon him with a cut...* - Paulus Hector Mair

From the "Low Guard True", the false edge is used to deflect the attack aside as seen in the prior technique from the "Low Guard False". In all the variations, the saber is held low and an attack is invited toward the head. This attack is deflected aside with the true or false edge of the saber. If needed, a passing step backward is used to create distance. While the opponent attempts to recover from the deflection, deliver an attack, passing forward if needed.

LOW GUARD DEFLECTION

Red waits in the "Low Guard False." When white attacks, red makes a strong deflection using the false edge of his saber. Red follows up with a cut at white's head before white can recover.

COUNTER TO A BEAT

When an opponent attempts to beat, it requires a tempo. From the "Middle Guard," when the opponent performs the beat against your blade, respond by performing an inside wrist moulinet, cutting from left-to-right, to void it. The moulinet strikes at the opponent's arm, which is exposed when their beat misses its target.

Another variation is from the "High Extended Guard." When the opponent attempts to beat the saber aside, withdraw the arm into the "High Retracted Guard." As the opponent's beat misses, follow up with a cut to the head.

Both of these variations rely on the same concept seen in voiding. The opponent misses their target and is vulnerable to a counter-attack while they recover.

Counter to a beat (Part 1)

White and Red stand in the "Middle Guard." White attempts to beat aside red's sword.

COUNTER TO A BEAT (PART 2)

After white attempts to beat aside red's saber, red performs an inside wrist moulinet to avoid the attempted beat. Red delivers the cut to white's exposed arm before he can recover from the missed beat.

Disarm

The sforzo strikes the opponent's sword with force in order to make the opponent drop it, or to deflect it from its position...In the disarmament, the opponent's sword receives the blow from the side opposite the palm of the hand, and vice versa for that of the deviation. - Settimo Del Frate

This method of disarming an opponent is a difficult technique, that is best described as a beat that has the potential to disarm an opponent. Engage the opponent's blade lightly to the inside. Then perform a simple cut directed at the false edge of the opponent's saber. The strike will act as the force behind a lever to pop the sword from the opponent's grasp. The quote above comes from a 19th century manual, but the concept is relevant for the 17th century because the same concept can apply.

DISARM (PART 1)

White and red stand in the "Middle Guard." Red brings his saber lightly against the inside of white's blade.

Disarm (Part 2)

Red has brought his saber to rest lightly on the inside of white's blade. Red then performs a cut that slides sharply down the length of white's saber. The force of the cut is directed against the false edge of white's saber and helps to pop it free from white's hand.

GRIPS

If he strikes straight at you from above like this and you stand with your left foot forward, strike a similar one and while striking grab his right hand with your left. Thus you catch him and can send the Schaitelhaw to his head. - Paulus Hector Mair

This technique involves responding to a cut with a cut, while either already standing left-foot forward or passing so as to become left-foot forward. The left hand can then grasp the opponent's wrist to control his sword.

Another variation.

The knight has performed an inside parry, then, lunging in, and using his opponent's effort to deliver his strike, he took the grip in the way shown. - Antonio Marcelli

This technique delivers a beat to the opponent's sword. Once the opponent's blade is displaced, perform a lunge, while both grabbing the opponent's wrist with your left hand and cutting them in the head with your sword.

Another variation.

If when you cut in to him, inside his blade, and he would quickly cut after you to the outside, thus step with your right foot well into him, and displace his strike nearly with the strong of your blade, as soon as his strike touches on your blade, then with your left hand under your right arm, grab away his right arm, quickly cut just then the Quarta from your left side, and from the outside to his right jaw... - Sebastian Heussler

This technique is a quick response when an opponent attempts a counter-cut to your outside. Lunge forward and defend with a hanging parry. The left hand reaches under the hanging parry to grasp the opponent's wrist. With the wrist secure, the opponent can then be cut.

GRIP (PART 1)

White and red stand in the "Middle Guard." White cuts at red, and in response, red cuts hard into white's attack to deflect it. This is similar to a beat.

GRIP (PART 2)

Having cut into white's cut, and deflecting white's sword aside, red passes forward and with his left hand grabs white's wrist before white can recover. Red is free to thrust or cut as is needed.

GRIP (ANOTHER VARIATION PART 1)

White and red stand in the "Middle Guard." White performs an attack, either a thrust or a cut. Red delivers a strong beat to drive white's sword to red's left (white's right).

GRIP (ANOTHER VARIATION PART 2)

After beating white's attack to the left, red lunges forward and with his left hand grips white's wrist. With white's weapon secured, red is free to cut or thrust as is needed.

GRIP (ANOTHER VARIATION PART 1)

Red and white stand in the "Middle Guard." White performs a cut directed at red's outside. Red moves into an inside hanging parry to intercept the attack.

GRIP (ANOTHER VARIATION PART 2)

Having intercepted white's attack with a hanging parry, red passes forward and reaches his left hand under his own sword and grips white's arm. Red twists and pulls down on the arm. His saber is now free to thrust or cut as is needed.

THE RIGHT AND WRONG TIME TO ATTACK

When fencing, there is a right time and a wrong time to attack. The goal is to hit and not be hit, and so attacks must be conducted with safety in mind.

WRONG TIME

Red makes a simple cut to white's head, while white is in the process of attacking with an arm moulinet. This is a bad time for red to attack. While red is likely to hit first, he is also likely to be hit a moment later by a much more powerful attack. It is not martially sound to launch an attack as the opponent is in the process of attacking, without a means to avoid being struck.

Red is cutting into white's side, while white is cutting at red's head. This "high for low" trade is martially unsound.

Wrong Time

Red makes a cut into white's side while white is performing an arm moulinet. Red might be able to form a "High Extended Guard" after his cut and be safe, but he is just as likely to end up with his sword trapped under white's arm. This is an unsafe attack.

Red thrusts while white is attacking with an arm moulinet. It is not martially sound to thrust in this situation because white will probably finish delivering his cut after being hit.

RIGHT TIME

Red makes a simple cut to white's hand as white prepares an arm moulinet. This is martially sound, because such an attack is intended not only to hit first, but also to hit white in a vulnerable area: the wrist. Furthermore, in this case, red attacks as white raises his arm, in an attempt to wound his opponent and shut down white's attack early.

Red has cut into the outside of white's wrist, moving laterally left as he does so. This is a good time to attack because red wounds white's wrist, which should be enough to end the fight. For added safety, red has moved off the line to try and void any counter-attack.

RIGHT TIME

Red cuts at white's head as white is in the process of changing guards. This is a good time to attack. White cannot do two things at once, so while he changes guards he is struck and cannot do anything about it.

Red attacks while white is in motion. This is a good time to attack. White will find it very difficult to defend, let alone attack, while his foot is in motion.

STARZEWSKI'S GUARDS IN ACTION

Starzewski describes several guards, which he calls Stances, to use during a fight. From the onset to the engagement, he has different positions the fencer should assume.

The guards are Initial, Facing and Engaging, followed by a guard each for Cutting, Defending and Retreating.

"The Italian would sneakily use his dagger, the Frenchman openly attack with a smallsword, and the Swede or the German, or some other foreigner, would thrust with his straight blade. The Pole, however, would use his saber-armed hand on the head and the nose and the ears of his opponent."
- Michał Starzewski

INITIAL

Red is in the "Initial Stance" of Starzewski. He awaits his opponent, with his saber near his right leg, with the majority of his weight supported by his left foot.

FACING

As white approaches, red bends his knees and raises his saber so that he is looking at white from under his guard. He is now in the "Facing Stance."

Engaging

The "Engaging Stance" of Starzewski is very similar to the "Facing Stance." Red is able to lean forward and backwards as needed and is ready to attack soon as soon as he sees an opening.

Cutting

The "Cutting Stance" of Starzewski springs from the "Engaging Stance." Red lunges forward and delivers a wrist moulinet at his opponent's hand or core (head or body). After delivering a cut, red will return to the "Facing Stance."

Defending

Starzewski's "Defending Stance" is the same as the "Facing Stance," but red sinks lower on the knees and is ready to offer his point to white's face.

Retreating

Red is in Starzewski's "Retreating Stance" which is like the "Defending Stance," but even lower on the knees. Starzewski describes it as if looking at the sun from under the saber and warding off attacks. If a fighter is pressed too hard, Starzewski suggests lateral movement and a counter-attack.

Dussack Plays

The dussack is generally a wooden training sword that was used in the 16th century and beyond, for which we have many German treatises. The nature of the dussack is similar to that of the Polish saber, and much of our inspiration on the use of the saber came from selected dussack plays.

The following are examples of dussack concepts and plays.

THE BOGEN

One of the guards used in dussack that is similar to the "High Extended Guard," but in this case the point is directed at the hip or lower body of the opponent.

"An experienced old dog feels the grip of his saber in his hand and knows how to spin it well, with skill and power."
- Michał Starzewski

ABSETZEN

If he strikes to your right arm like this and you also stand in the Absetzen with your right foot set forward, set it aside with your long edge. Then immediately follow outward with your left leg, grab with your left hand at his right, and strike him to his head. - Paulus Hector Mair

An Absetzen is where you set aside an attack, and respond accordingly. In this example, red offers her arm as bait for an attack. She parries, passes and grabs her opponent's arm.

ENTRUSTHAU AGAINST THE OBERHAU

He then strikes to your upper opening, so follow outward with your right foot and go with your Duseggen up over your head so that the long edge is turned upward and his strike is displaced. Then immediately strike quickly with the Zwirch to his right ear. - Paulus Hector Mair

In this play, black tempts a strike to his head. When red attempts to cut, black responds by passing and using the false edge of his dussack to deflect her attack aside. He then passes and strikes the right side of her head before she can recover properly.

TWO POSITIONS FROM WHICH THE CREIZHAW PROCEEDS

When you come together at the closing, it happens with these positions: your right foot is set forward, your Dussack held with the hilt near your right knee with your left hand behind near the point (left side of illustration). He then strikes to your opening from above, so go up with your Dussack above your head such that your left foot is set forward. Thus his strike is displaced. Then immediately strike with a doubled Creizhaw (Cross-Cut) to his head.

If he strikes you double like this from above and you have your Dussack at your right leg with the long edge directed at your opponent, the point directed at the ground, and your right foot set forward (right side of illustration), shove this away crosswise with your short edge. Then immediately set upon him with a cut from below on his right arm and grab his right elbow with your left hand so that you shove him from you. Follow outward with your left leg and strike him to the upper opening. - Paulus Hector Mair

From these two positions it is possible to deflect an incoming strike, with the true or false edge, and to respond with a cross cut to the opponent's head.

QUICK CUT

Mark thus when you stand before one in the Bow, and he will not cut so pull upwards into the Watch as if you would cut from high especially if he does nothing, wind in the air and cut with the long edge from under to his right arm quickly and jerk the Dussack again around to your left shoulder, from there cut a defense strike through his right, to the arm or above the arm through to his face, and then cut Cross or a Driving cut.

Item If he cuts from above in the before, thus displace upwards towards your left and cut through quickly from your left to his right it is under or above the Dussack thus you come with your Dussack beside your right side, from there cut again athwart from under with the long edge strongly through his arm, or if he cuts against your strike so that your Dussack comes to your left shoulder, cut away directly from the over line. - Joachim Meyer

The first part of this technique involves using a feint against a person in the "Bow Guard." The "Bow Guard" is the same as the *Bogen* of Mair and is similar to the "High Extended Guard."

AGAINST THE BOW (PART 1)

The fencer on the right feints a high attack against the fencer on the left who is in the "Bow Guard." Before the dussack hits, the fencer on the right turns his wrist so he ends up cutting under his opponent's dussack, beating it aside.

Against the Bow (Part 2)

Having cut under his opponent's dussack and beating it aside, the fencer on the right draws his arm back and delivers a cut to the fencer on the left's arm before he can recover.

A GOOD DEVICE FROM THE STIER

If you encounter one who is in the Slice how this figure shows, thus step and cut from your right crooked under his right arm through so that you connect near his knuckles with the crooked point, the other take him strongly away with the flat upwards through his right arm from your left, so that your weapon again flies around your head, with this thrust over his right arm to the face, if he defends this, thus cut him to the face.

Item *In the onset cut in with Long edge strongly through his face, so that your dussack again shoots over your head athwart to the displacement from your right, step instantly and quickly with your left around his right and cut him Crooked over his right arm to the head if he defends, thus cut him forwards to the face or cut him crooked to the left at the head.* - Joachim Meyer

The fencer on the left is in the "Stier Guard" which is similar to the "High Retracted Guard." From here, she can perform a pass forward and use the false edge of her dussack to beat aside her opponent's dussack. From there she can continue with the motion and deliver strikes to the right or left of her opponent, depending on how he recovers from the initial beat.

Gear

There are a variety of resources for those interested in drilling and sparring with the Polish saber. Below are some sample outfits as well as the information and websites of various retailers.[217]

Zen Warrior Armory "Armored Gloves"

Zen Warrior Armory Mask

Hard Elbow Pads

PBT Coaching Jacket

Dave Baker Saber - Modern guard

Purple Heart "Padded Gloves"

Absolute Force HEMA Mask

Mizuno Batter Elbow Guard

Zen Warrior Fencing Jacket

Dave Baker Saber- Modern guard

217   The author and the Phoenix Society do not endorse any product as safe for the purposes of sparring. Sparring and the safety of such is solely in the hands of the participant. The gear suggestions are only that and no amount of gear will entirely eliminate the risk of injury. Sparring should only be done in a controlled environment with safety being a top concern.

Purple Heart "Padded Gloves"

Absolute Force HEMA Mask

Leather Forearm Bracers

Leather Gorget

Jessica Finley Wrestling Jacket

External Cod Piece

Dave Baker Saber - Historical guard

Football Sports Gloves

Absolute Force HEMA Mask

Leather Forearm Bracers

Soft Elbow Pads

Leather Gorget

Sweater with T-Shirt

Wojciech Szanek Saber - Modern guard

Riot Gloves

3 Weapon Fencing Mask

Hard Shoulder/Elbow Pads

SPES Jacket

External Cod Piece

Purple Heart Synthetic Saber

Absolute Force: Absolute Force, found at www.AbsoluteForceSports.com, supplies protective gear for HEMA (Historical European Martial Arts). Masks, jackets and throat-protection are available.

Corsair's Wares is the online retail division for Triquetra Services (Scotland), a historical education charity that seeks to promote and further the study of European history through the medium of the historical, martial and creative arts. Their online shop specializes in providing high quality equipment for different sections of the historical hobbyist market, from some of the best suppliers in Europe. All of the proceeds from every sale go straight towards helping the charity fund its educational programs for the local, national and international communities.

www.corsairs-wares.com

Hollywood Combat Center: Dave Baker, from www.HollywoodCombatCenter.com can custom design both steel Polish sabers for cutting, or aluminum Polish sabers for sparring. We suggest that for sparring, modern shell-guards are used so as to keep the hand safe.

Polish Hussar Supply: Eric Jadaszewski sells a variety of 17th century Polish equipment at www. PolishHussarSupply.com. Armor, display swords, clothing and more can be purchased. Eric is also the author of a guide to reenacting the 17th century in Poland.

Purple Heart Armory: Purple Heart, found at www.WoodenSwords.com sells affordable synthetic sabers that can simulate Polish sabers.

SPES: SPES Historical Fencing Gear sells a variety of protective gear, ranging from gloves, to jackets, to helmets. They also carry foam sabers, which are good for light drills or youths. They can be found at http://histfenc.us

Resources

Michael Chidester went beyond providing just guidance to the project. When I needed a scan of the Middle Guard from Thomas Rowlandson, Michael not only found the image I needed, he went to the University and scanned it for me. Additionally, Chidester is the director of Wiktenauer, the largest online resource of HEMA treatises. With tireless effort, he has made Wiktenauer an invaluable resource for anyone interested in historical martial arts.

Wiktenauer can be found at www.Wiktenauer.com.

The HEMA Alliance is an organization that supports, promotes and encourages the study, practice and re-creation of Historical European Martial Arts. This work would not have been possible without the interest and support of the Alliance community.

The HEMA Alliance can be found at HemaAlliance.com.

HROARR is an *independent, neutral meeting ground* and *resource site* dedicated to the Historical European Martial Arts community.
They are provided by Gothenburg Historical Fencing School.

Access the site at HROARR.com.

Jeffery Lord was incredibly kind to the project, providing resources without charge and asking for only one thing in return: that others read the manuscripts he has helped preserve and put online.

A variety of resources, including Antonio Marcelli's *Regole della Scherma*, 1686, can be found at the Raymond J. Lord Collection at www.UMass.edu/Renaissance/Lord/Collection.html.

The Phoenix Society of Historical Swordsmanship have provided a condensed, free PDF of the Polish Saber Project that can be found at http://Tinyurl.com/Freesaber

The Phoenix Society can be found at www.phoenixswordclub.com.

Glossary

Bohdan Chmielnicki	Leader of the Ukrainian rebellion
Brzytewki	Type of sword
Czajka	River boat
Ciężar	Weight of a sword
Czekan	Type of war-hammer
Delia	Type of coat
Demeszki	Type of sword
Karabela	Type of sword
Karwanierzy	Type of soldier
Kieł	The fang, a part of the hilt
Kłącz	Knuckleguard of the sword
Kord	Saber
Kontusz	Type of coat
Michał Wiśniowiecki	Polish King
nadziak	Type of war-hammer
nyżek	Cut from below to the right, aimed at the stomach
nyżkiem	Cut from below to the right, aimed at the stomach
obuch	Type of war-hammer
odlew	Moulinet from left to right
odpowiedź	A challenge
oręże	Type of heavy straight sword
pałasz	Type of heavy straight sword
pałasik	Lighter version of the *pałasz*
palcat	Training stick
palcaty	A pair of training sticks or a fencing game
paragrafy	Articles of law in reference to a cut to the face
podajność	How a blade's strong and weak operate
podlew	A low moulinet from left to right

rapcie	Elegant straps that held the saber's sheathe
rozprawa	A fight or duel
Rzeczpospolita Polska	The Commonwealth of the Polish Republic
scyzoryki	Type of sword
Sejm	The Commonwealth's Parliament
sejmik	Local Parliament
serpentyny	Type of sword
smyczki	Type of sword
szlachta	Noble
szlachcic	Nobility
stambułki	Turkish sword
szabla	Saber
szaszka	Type of Russian sword with no quillons
tasaki	Type of sword
w łąż	Cut from the left into the opponent's wrist
w łęg	Cut to the neck from the left
w trok	Cut to the opponent's left hip
waga	Mechanical nature of the sword
wkłącz	Cut to the opponent's palm
wkłęb	Cut to the opponent's right hip
wkiść	Cut from above into the opponent's wrist
wlew	A left to right cut into the opponent's neck
wlic	A high cut to the opponent's right cheek
wnik	A low cut from left to right into the opponent's hand
wpierś	A cut through the arm-pit into the chest
wprawa	Practice fencing or sparring
wręb	Powerful hack through the left arm to the body
wtrzon	A cut to the opponent's fingers
wzerk	A high cut to the opponent's left eye
Zaporizhian	Cossacks from central Ukraine
żupan	A long garment worn under a coat but over a shirt

Pronunciations

by Daria Izdebska

This little pronunciation guide is supposed to aid American and British English speakers with the pronunciation of Polish words. As such, it is a necessary approximation, for ease of use with this book.

CONSONANTS

Most consonants are pronounced somewhat similarly to English/American (e.g. m, d, b, p, t, etc.).

Such as:

kh – as the "ch" in the Scottish lo**ch**

zh – as the "s" in mea**s**ure

ts – as in **ts**ar or **ts**unami

There is a difference in Polish between "sz" and "ś" / 'si', and between "ch" and "ć" / "ci," that cannot be reflected in English spelling as English does not distinguish between the two sounds. The Polish "sz" is like a harder English/American "sh" in **sh**oe, and "cz" is like a harder English/American "ch" in **ch**eck. The "ś" and "ć" are similar, but softened (essentially more "ee"-like), hence, occasionally the "ee" marks that.

The combination "dż" does not occur in the words below, but is essentially like the English/American "j" in **j**am. However, "dź" (with a slightly different mark above the "z") is its softened counterpart (occurring in one word in the glossary), is pronounced a little like the sound at the start of **ge**nie, and is indicated below as "je."

Vowels

Whenever an "h" comes after a vowel it denotes a short vowel, for instance:

eh – as in t**e**nt or in s**e**t

ah – as in h**a**t

aw – as in th**ough**t, or h**o**t (with a British accent), but not a long sound as in **aw**esome

uh – as in f**oo**t

Sometimes the "h" is omitted in places where it is not necessary, because English/American would not use a long vowel or diphthong anyway (as in "ey" in s**ey**m).

The Polish vowel "y" does not have an English/American equivalent. It is a little similar to the "i" in **i**s or in t**i**p (which is a much shorter vowel). At the ends of words the "ih" represents the sound.

The following vowel combinations are pronounced:

ee – as in pl**ea**

oo – as in f**oo**d

For the nasalized Polish vowels "ę" or "ą," a "n" comes after the vowel ("ehn" or "ohn"), which makes them similar enough, though it is again an approximation.

The words are marked in italics where the stress is supposed to go in each word.

Bohdan Chmielnicki	[*Baw*-kh-dahn Khmyel-*neets*-kee]
brzytewki	[bzhih-*tehv*-kee]
czajka	[*chah*-y-kah]
ciężar	[*chee-en*-zhahr]
czekan	[*check*-ahn]
delia	[*dehl*-yah]
demeszki	[deh-*mehsh*-kee]
karabela	[car-ah-*beh*-lah]
karwanierzy	[car-vah-*nee-eh*-zhy]
Kieł	[*kyeh*-w]
kłącz	[*kwonch*]
kord	[*cawrd*]
kontusz	[*kawn*-tuhsh]
Michał Wiśniowiecki	[*Mee*-hahw Vee-shnyaw-*vee-ets*-kee]
nadziak	[nah-*dzee-ahk*]
nyżek	[*nih*-zheck]
nyżkiem	[*nihzh*-kee-ehm]
obuch	[*aw*-bookh]
odlew	[*awd*-lev]
odpowiedź	[od-*paw*-vee-eh-je]
oręże	[oh-*ren*-zhih]
pałasz	[*pah*-wah-sh]
pałasik	[pah-*wah*-sheek]
palcat	[*pahl*-tsaht]
palcaty	[pahl-*tsaht*-ih]
paragrafy	[pah-rah-*grah*-fih]
podajność	[poh-*dahy*-noh-sh-ch]
podlew	[*pawd*-lev]
rapcie	[*rahp*-chee-eh]
rozprawa	[roz-*prah*-vah]
Rzeczpospolita Polska	[zh-etch-paws-*paw*-lee-tah *Pawl*-skah]
scyzoryki	[s-tsih-zaw-*rih*-kee]
Sejm	[*seym*]
sejmik	[*sey*-meek]
serpentyny	[sehr-pehn-*tih*-nih]

smyczki	[*smih*-tch-kee]
szlachta	[*shlakh*-tah]
szlachcic	[*shlakh*-cheets]
stambułki	[stahm-*boow*-kee]
szabla	[*shah*-blah]
szaszka	[*shahsh*-kah]
tasaki	[tah-*sah*-kee]
w łąż	[v-*wonzh*]
w łęg	[v-*weng*]
w trok	[f-*trock*]
waga	[*vah*-gah]
wkłącz	[v-*kwon*-ch]
wkłęb	[f-*kwenb*]
wkiść	[f-*kee*-sh-ch]
wlew	[v-*lev*]
wlic	[v-*leets*]
wnik	[v-*neek*]
wpierś	[f-*pee-ehr*-sh]
wprawa	[f-*prah*-vah]
wręb	[v-*renb*]
wtrzon	[f-tsh-*on*]
wzerk	[v-*zerck*]
Zaporizhian	[Zah-paw-*rih-zh*-ee-an]
żupan	[*zhoo*-pahn]

Acknowledgements

Richard Marsden, the author, has been involved in historical fencing for two decades and is a founder of the Phoenix Society of Historical Swordsmanship and he was President of the HEMA Alliance. He has earned medals in a variety of Historical European Martial Arts tournaments and his students have done the same. He earned his Bachelor's degree in Secondary Education at ASU West, and his Masters degree in Military Studies at AMU. He is the author of several books and short-stories and has a wife who tolerates his many eccentricities.

Keith Farrell, the editor of this volume, is one of the senior instructors for the Academy of Historical Arts, based in Scotland. He teaches HEMA professionally, often at international events, and has an interest in coaching instructors to become better teachers. He is the co-author of the *AHA German Longsword Study Guide* and has been a member of HEMAC since 2011.

Daria Izdebska, our lead researcher, is currently a doctoral student at Glasgow University, finishing her degree in Old English. When not engaged in academia or teaching students, she researches the cross-cutting art of Polish saber. She has translated Starzewski's treatise into English, as well as some other works dealing with Polish saber, both modern and historical.

Kevin Maurer is a member of the Meyer Freyfechter Guild and a practitioner of HEMA for 10 years. He currently holds the rank of Senior Research Scholar within his guild. His primary focus has been on the physical reconstruction of the fighting art of Joachim Meyer, including all the weapons, "from the longest to the shortest."

Jerzy Miklaszewski started his 19 years of martial art experience with a variety of Eastern martial arts. He met fellow European martial arts enthusiasts, where under harsh, unyielding and implacable training conditions, he started to use all his previously gained knowledge. After a few years of sparring, Jerzy started winning at tournaments. That is when he, with his fellow senior instructor created the Silk Fencing team, drawing from past experiences to rediscover Western martial arts. Jerzy provided work, photos, and tremendous support to this project.

Keith P. Myers has been involved in martial arts of one sort or another for the last 30 years. He became involved in HEMA in 2000 and is the author of *Medieval Hand-to-Hand Combat*, which was self-published in 2002. Keith started out in the "early American" era with Bowie Knife, Tomahawk, Bayonet, Saber/broadsword, and Bare-knuckle Boxing. He also spent time studying the German Longsword, Sword & Buckler methods of I.33, the Regimental Broadsword methods of Henry Angelo, and the methods of the Bolognese school of swordsmanship. He is a self-taught translator and has translated the wrestling manuals of Hans Wurm and Fabian von Auerswald, the fencing manual of Jakob Sutor, and large portions of Paulus Hector Mair's "*Opus*". He is a member of the Meyer Frei Fechter Guild and a lifetime member of the HEMA Alliance.

Reinier van Noort is the main instructor and founder of the School for Historical Fencing Arts. He started modern (foil) fencing in 2003, but in the summer of 2005 he was introduced to Medieval European Martial Arts, which changed his life forever. From 2005 until 2010, Reinier trained fighting with the longsword as well as with other medieval European weapons with several groups in the Netherlands, and from 2007 he was increasingly active as a trainer with one of these groups. From 2008 until 2011 Reinier has also trained Kadochnikov Systema. After making the first English translation of Bruchius's *Grondige Beschryvinge van de Edele ende Ridderlijcke Scherm- ofte Wapen-konste* in October 2009, Reinier got very interested in rapier fencing, and since January 2010 he has been researching, training and teaching the Art of Fencing described by Bruchius in practice. In addition, Reinier has produced a number of articles, transcriptions and translations.

Jake Norwood is an internationally-known competitor and instructor in Historical European Martial Arts (HEMA), with over a dozen medals from national and international full-contact competitions in Longsword, Military Saber, Dussack, and target cutting since 2010. A multi-tour combat veteran of the 101st Airborne, Jake combines the training regimen and psychological toughness of the modern warrior to the reconstruction and physical application of Europe's traditional fighting arts. As an instructor, Jake has presented his aggressive, dynamic approach to Kunst des Fechtens, or the Art of Fighting, at workshops and conferences across Germany, Sweden Canada, and the United States. He is the head instructor at Maryland Kunst des Fechtens and Capital Kunst des Fechtens, both in the Washington, D.C. area. His students are among the top competitors in the U.S. HEMA tournament scene. Jake is a current board member and the former president of the HEMA Alliance.

Carlo Parisi started practicing HEMA in 1998, became a member of HEMAC in 2003. His main interests are the military saber, the English backsword, the spada da lato, the dagger, the spadancia, the spadroon, the smallsword. He taught workshops on these and other subjects at HEMA events, posted articles and translations on the HEMAC site and joined an editorial project managed by Fabrice Cognot in 2006. Now he runs a small group in which every member was invited to do research as well as practice.

John Patterson is co-founder of the Phoenix Society of Historical Swordsmanship. He is an accomplished fencer with wins and placements in all of North America in longsword, wrestling and rapier. John has also taught at numerous events. His students have routinely performed well. He, along with Richard Marsden, is co-author of Savage Worlds: War of the Worlds: The Remains.

Lee Smith is the head of Blood and Iron, a premier HEMA school based in Vancouver Canada. Lee Smith has won numerous tournaments in many weapon systems including longsword, rapier and single-stick. He is a vaunted instructor and his students routinely win medals and teach seminars as well. Lee has also directed numerous tournaments. He was also the HEMA Alliance Curriculum Director for two terms. Blood and Iron has been a major presence in all of North America and Europe bringing excellent fencing, teaching and professionalism to the HEMA community. Lee is a dedicated husband to Nicole, who assists him in his martial ventures. Nicole is also a skilled fencer and dedicated teacher and a pillar of Blood and Iron.

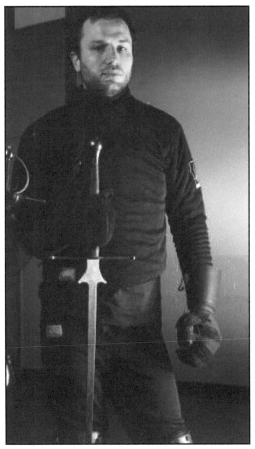

Piermarco Terminiello is an historical fencer and researcher. He was born in London, and grew up between Sorrento, Italy and the South of England where he currently resides. He studies historical fencing with the School of the Sword, and is a member of the Historical European Martial Arts Coalition (HEMAC), an association of researchers from across Europe. His research interest is focused on sixteenth and seventeenth century Italian swordplay. In 2013, he and Joshua Pendragon translated and released the "lost" book of Giganti. He has enjoyed success as a competitive fencer, winning a number of international competitions in the disciplines of single rapier, rapier and dagger, and sword and buckler.

ADDITIONAL THANKS

Jessica Marcarelli is a freelance writer and photographer. She wanted to be a pirate but, lacking a sturdy ship and the crew to man it, she settled for the aforesaid. She lives in Phoenix, Arizona with her husband, one precocious cat, and enough books to cause a small avalanche. Her photography portfolio can be found at https://www.flickr.com/photos/jessicashley.

Erik Atikinson for wonderful Polish costumes.

Ksenia Kozhevnikova, Mariana López-Rodríguez, and Miandra T.Thomas for copying of plates.

Andrzej Mikiciak for providing as well as making the saber on the cover. Contact him for work at mikiciak@poczta.onet.pl.

Henry Snider for layout and cover design. Read his prose or contact him at henrysnider.com.

Additional Resources

Jędrzej Kitowicz, translated by Daria Izdebska.

"On Customs and Traditions in the Reign of Augustus III"

http://www.historical-academy.co.uk/files/research/daria-izdebska/Kitowicz%20-%20Customs%20and%20Traditions.pdf

Richard Marsden, Keith Farrell and others.

"Polish Saber: A Basic Guide"

http://Tinyurl.com/Freesaber

Joachim Meyer, translated by Kevin Maurer.

"Meyer 1560"

https://sites.google.com/site/jochimmeyer1560/

Bartoz Sienawski, translated by Daria Izdebska.

"The Saber's Many Travels"

http://www.hroarr.com/the-sabers-many-travels-the-origins-of-the-cross-cutting-art/

Michał Starzewski, translated by Daria Izdebska.

"On Fencing"

http://www.historical-academy.co.uk/files/research/daria-izdebska/Michal%20Starzewski%20-%20On%20Fencing.pdf Starzewski Online

Jerzy Miklaszewski demonstrates how the study of this incomplete art continues. He has taken an image from Heinrich von Günterode and with what little translation there is, tried to interpret it.

(Image copied from plate by Miranda T. Thomas listed as Gunderodt)

http://tinyurl.com/SaberReconstruction

230

IMAGES

Territorial Changes of Poland

http://commons.wikimedia.org/wiki/File:Territorial_changes_of_Poland_1699.jpg   Poland 1699
Released to the Public Domain by author.

CANNONS

http://commons.wikimedia.org/wiki/File:Benningk_1669.jpg Cannons
Public Domain PD-Art -Old/Copyright Expired.

MANUAL OF THE MUSKETEER

http://commons.wikimedia.org/wiki/File:Manual_of_the_Musketeer,_17th_Century.jpg   Musket
Drill
Public Domain PD-Art -Old/Copyright Expired.

GDANSK SKETCH

http://commons.wikimedia.org/wiki/File:Gdansk_in_18th_c.jpg Gdansk sketch
Public Domain PD-Art -Old/Copyright Expired.

SEJM UNDER THE REIGN OF SIGISMUND III VASA

http://commons.wikimedia.org/wiki/File:Polish_Sejm_under_the_reign_of_Sigismund_III_Vasa.
JPG Sigismund III
Public Domain PD-Art -Old/Copyright Expired.

OATH OF CASIMIR

http://commons.wikimedia.org/wiki/File:Sluby_Jana_Kazimierza_2.jpg Oath of Casimir
Public Domain PD-Art -Old/Copyright Expired.

JOHN III SOBIESKI

http://www.pinakoteka.zascianek.pl/Kossak_Jul/Images/Na_Kahlenbergu.jpg   John III Sobieski
Public Domain PD-Art -Old/Copyright Expired.

POLISH HUSSAR

http://commons.wikimedia.org/wiki/File:Polish_Hussar_half-armour_Winged_Riders.jpg
CC that is Share and Remix and Attribute but NOT Share Alike as of 7-28-2013 by Bazylek100.

TURKISH WEAPONS OF THE 17TH CENTURY

http://commons.wikimedia.org/wiki/File:Turkey.Bodrum077.jpg
Creative Commons attribution Share-Alike.

SKARGI'S SERMON

http://en.wikipedia.org/wiki/File:Kazanie_Skargi.jpg Sermon,
Public Domain PD-Art Old/Expired

POLISH NOBLE

http://commons.wikimedia.org/wiki/File:Norblin_-_Avocat_polonais.jpg Polish Patron
Public Domain Art

GOLUHOV COSTUME

http://commons.wikimedia.org/wiki/File:Goluhov-costume-tableau.png 1620 Costume
Public Domain Art

1630 COSTUME

http://commons.wikimedia.org/wiki/File:Portret_Stanis%C5%82awa_T%C4%99czy%C5%84skie
go.jpg 1630 costume
Public Domain Art

ELECTION DIET, 1697

http://en.wikipedia.org/wiki/Free_election,_1697#mediaviewer/File:Altomonte_Election_Diet_
in_1697.jpg
Public Domain Art

POLISH NOBILITY

http://commons.wikimedia.org/wiki/File:Polish_nobility_in_1697.JPG Almonte Palcaty
Public Domain Art

AN OUTLINE OF THE RULES OF FENCING, WITH SKETCHES, IN FIVE PARTS

http://www.reenactor.ru/ARH/Drill/Pravila_Fext_1843.pdf
Public Domain Art

MAYER WOODCUT

http://dariocaballeros.blogspot.com/2011/01/lucas-mayer-woodcuts-1595-96-warfare-in.html
Public Domain PD-Art Old/Expired

Rowlandson, Thomas, 1799. *Hungarian and Highland Broadsword*. HEW 9.13.22, Harry Elkins
Widener Collection, Harvard University, courtesy Michael Chidester.

All other art and photos provided by the author, Ksenia Kozhevnikova, Mariana López-Rodríguez,
Jessica Marcarelli, Miranda T. Thomas, translators, researchers as well as by the Arizona Renaissance Festival.

Bibliography

Boziewicz, Władysław. *Polski kodeks honorowy 1919*. literat.ug.edu

literat.ug.edu/honor/ (accessed 7-23-2014).

Brzezinski, Richard. *Polish Armies 1569-1696* (1). London: Osprey Publishing, 1987.

Chandler, Jeanry. Interview with Richard Marsden. Facebook Interview. Phoenix, July 3, 2013.

Chidester, Michael. Interview with Richard Marsden. Facebook Interview. Phoenix, September 20, 2013.

Childs, John. *Warfare in the Seventeenth Century*. London: Cassell, 2001.

Davies, Norman. *God's Playground*. New York: Columbia University Press, 1982.

Ferro, Capo. Trans. William Wilson. *Gran Simulacro dell'Arte e dell'Uso della Scherma*. mac9.ucc. nau.edu/manuscripts/

http://mac9.ucc.nau.edu/manuscripts/pcapo/ (accessed 5-5-2013).

Forgeng, Jeffrey. *The Art of Combat: A German Martial Arts Treatise of 1570*. New York: Palgrave MacMillan, 2006.

Gordon, Anthony. *A Treatise on the Science of Defence for the Sword, Bayonet, and Pike in Close Action 1805*. Uckfield: The Naval and Military Press, 2013.

Holzman, Christopher. *The Art of the Dueling Sabre*. New York: SKA Swordplay Books, 2011.

Horse Guards, *Infantry Sword Exercise 1842*. Norfolk: Wyvern Media, 2010.

Henning, Erhardus. Trans. Reinier van Noort. *Kurtze jedoch gründliche Unterrichtung vom Hiebfechten*.

http://bruchius.com/docs/Henning%20translation%20by%20RvN.pdf (accessed 5-5-2013).

Heussler, Sebastian. Trans. Kevin Maurer. *New Kůnstlich Fechtbuch*. www.Friefechter.com

http://freifechter.com/heussler.pdf (accessed 5-5-2013).

Johnson, Lonnie R. *Central Europe*. New York: Oxford University Press, 1996.

Kiernan, V.G. *The Duel in European History*. Oxford: Oxford University Press, 1989.

Kitowicz, Jędrzej. Trans. Daria Izdebska. *On Customs and Traditions in the Reign of Augustus III*. www.historical-academy.co.uk

http://www.historical-academy.co.uk/files/research/daria-izdebska/Kitowicz%20-%20Customs%20and%20Traditions.pdf (accessed 5-5-2013).

Libieri, Fiore. Trans. Michael Chidester. *Flos Duellatorum*. www.wiktenauer.com

http://wiktenauer.com/wiki/Fiore_de%27i_Liberi (accessed 5-5-2013).

Leoni, Tom. *Art of Dueling*. Highland Village: Chivalry Press, 2005.

Leoni, Tom. *Venetian Rapier*. Wheaton: Freelance Academy Press, 2010.

Mair, Paulus Hector. Trans. Keith P Myers. *Opus Amplissimum de Arte Athletica*. www.wiktenauer. com

http://wiktenauer.com/wiki/Paulus_Hector_Mair (accessed 5-5-2013).

Manciolino, Antonio. Trans. Tom Leoni. *Opera Nova*. Wheaton: Freelance Academy Press, 2010.

Marcelli, Antonio. *The Rules of Fencing*. www.umass.edu/renaissance/lord

http://www.umass.edu/renaissance/lord/pdfs/Marcelli_1686.pdf (accessed 5-5-2013).

Maurer, Kevin. Interview with Richard Marsden. Facebook Interview. Phoenix, January 26, 2013.

Meyer, Joachim. Trans. Kevin Maurer. *Meyer 1560*. www.Friefechter.com. https://sites.google.com/site/jochimmeyer1560/ (accessed 5-5-2013).

Meyer, Joachim. *Joachim Meyer*. www.wiktenauer.com

http://wiktenauer.com/wiki/Joachim_Me%C3%BFer (accessed 5-5-2013).

Miedema, Aaraon Taylor. *Nicoletto Giganti's The School of the Sword*. Kingston: Legacy Books Press, 2014.

Milligen, John Gideon. *The History of Dueling*. London: Samuel Bently, 1841.

Pendragon, Joshua and Piermarco Terminiello. *The Lost Second Book of Nicoletto Giganti*. London: Vulpes, 2013.

Pasek, Jan Chryzostom. Trans. Catherine S. Leach. *Memoirs of the Polish Baroque*. Los Angeles: University of California Press, 1976.

Rector, Mark. Highland *Swordsmanship: Techniques of the Scottish Swordmasters*.Union City: Chivalry Bookshelf, 2001.

Schama, Simon. *Landscape and Memory Vintage*. New York: New York, 1995.

Silver, George. Trans. Paul Wagner. *Master of Defence: The Works of George Silver*. Boulder: Paladin Press, 2003.

Starzewski, Michał. Trans. Daria Izdebska. *On Fencing*. www.historical-academy.co.uk/ http://www.historical-academy.co.uk/files/research/daria-izdebska/Michal%20Starzewski%20-%20On%20Fencing.pdf (accessed 5-5-2013).

Sutor, Jacob. Trans. Kevin P. Myers. *New Illustrated Fechtbuch of 1612*. www.Friefechter.com

https://docs.google.com/file/d/0Bxqzt-jcOCFsT19Xa1Q2QXltWm8/edit?pli=1 (accessed 5-5-2013).

Tadeusz, Sulimirski. *The Sarmatians*. New York: Praeger Publishers, 1970.

Walters Art Gallery, *Land of the Winged Horsemen*. VHS, prod The Walters Art Gallery, Baltimore, Video, 1999.

Zabłocki, Wojciech. *Ciecia Prawdziwa Szabla*, Warsaw: Wydawnictwo sport i Turystyka, 1989.

Zabłocki, Wojciech. *Szable świata*. Warsaw: Wydawnictwo, 2011.

Index

Portrait of author by Ksenia Kozhevnikova of Blood and Iron